ANIMAL BEHAVIOR

Animal
Defenses

ANIMAL BEHAVIOR

Animal Communication
Animal Courtship
Animal Defenses
Animal Hunting and Feeding
Animal Life in Groups
Animal Migration

ANIMAL BEHAVIOR

Animal
Defenses

CHRISTINA WILSDON

CHELSEA HOUSE
PUBLISHERS

An imprint of Infobase Publishing

Animal Behavior: Animal Defenses

Copyright © 2009 by Infobase Publishing

Chelsea House
An imprint of Infobase Publishing
132 West 31st Street
New York NY 10001

Library of Congress Cataloging-in-Publication Data

Wilsdon, Christina.
  Animal defenses / Christina Wilsdon.
    p. cm. — (Animal behavior)
  Includes bibliographical references and index.
  ISBN 978-1-60413-089-8 (hardcover)
  ISBN 978-0-81608-512-5 (paperback)
  1. Animal defenses. I. Title. II. Series.
  QL759.W55 2009
  591.47—dc22 2008040116

Text design and composition by Kerry Casey
Cover design by Ben Peterson
Cover printed by Strategic Content Imaging, Secaucus, NJ
Book printed and bound by Strategic Content Imaging, Secaucus, NJ
Printed in the United States of America

This book is printed on acid-free paper.

All links and Web addresses were checked and verified to be correct at the time of publication. Because of the dynamic nature of the Web, some addresses and links may have changed since publication and may no longer be valid.

Caption: A thorny devil, native to Australia, is camouflaged in shades of desert browns and tans. The spikes on its body also help protect it from predators.

Contents

1

Avoiding Danger

A CHEETAH SKULKS through the tall grass of the African savannah. Head lowered, she stares intently at a herd of gazelles. Her spotted coat blends in with the dry grass, making her nearly invisible as she sneaks up on her **prey**.

The gazelles continue to graze. Between bites of grass, each one snaps up its head to check out its surroundings. Bright eyes scan the horizon. Ears swivel to pick up the slightest sound. Nostrils flare to sniff for the scent of a cheetah, lion, or other hungry **predator**.

Suddenly, a few gazelles snort and stamp their feet. The entire herd goes on high alert. The black bands that run down the gazelles' sides quiver, passing along the message: "Danger!" Then, some of the gazelles begin bouncing as if on pogo sticks. They spring high in the air with their backs arched and legs stiff. They land on all fours, and then leap again.

The cheetah pauses. The gazelles have seen her. It is impossible to launch a surprise attack now. The cheetah depends on one short-lived, startling burst of speed to chase down a gazelle. The gazelles, however, also run fast, hitting speeds of up to 40 miles (64 km) an hour—and they can keep up this speed much longer

This female springbok, a kind of antelope, bounces into the air with an arched back and stiff legs. This motion is called stotting or pronking. Springbok typically use it to show predators that they are fit and hard to catch. Research shows that cheetahs often avoid hunting stotting springbok.

than a cheetah can. Their odd jumping behavior, called stotting, signals to the cheetah, "We have seen you, so do not bother to chase us—we are strong and healthy and can outrun you."

If the cheetah is lucky, perhaps she will find a gazelle fawn hidden in the grass. However, the fawns have tawny coats and can lie still as a stone for a long time. Plus, the fawns' mothers are careful not to give the cheetah any clues as to where their young are hiding.

Like most wild animals, gazelles are always watching out for danger. Most often, that danger is another animal—in this case, a hungry cheetah. Even domestic animals, such as horses, sheep, and chickens, are on the alert for any threat to their safety. Being alert is the first step an animal takes to defend itself. It is one of many behaviors that animals use to survive in a world filled with predators.

Much of an animal's self-defense behavior comes from within it. Most animals are born "knowing" how to defend themselves. Scientists call this inborn knowledge instinct.

SELF-DEFENSE

Over millions of years, the many different kinds, or species, of animals have developed ways of defending themselves. Animals might use protective colors, sharp spines, and excellent hearing. An animal has its defensive tools at the ready all the time, whether or not it is in danger. They are known as **primary defenses**. The gazelle's primary defenses include its horns, its keen senses, and its speed. A gazelle fawn's primary defenses include its ability to lie still and its concealing coat color.

An animal's primary defenses are backed up by behaviors known as **secondary defenses**. The animal uses its secondary defenses when it confronts a predator. A gazelle uses secondary defenses when it stamps, stots, and runs away—or if it is caught by a cheetah or other predator.

Gazelle fawns use the most basic form of self-defense: avoid being noticed. Like the fawns, many animals evade detection by hiding, freezing, or blending in with their habitat. This is called **crypsis** (*crypsis* comes from a Greek word that means "hidden.")

LYING LOW

Many animals hide to avoid being noticed. Turn over a stone or stir a pile of leaves to reveal a world of hidden creatures: a worm squirming in the sudden burst of light, a rolled-up pill bug, a centipede quickly scurrying out of sight, tiny springtails, and even tinier mites. Trees and other plants harbor animals seeking hideaways. Insects hide under leaves, along stems, and under scraps of bark. Pale trails winding through a leaf show where the larvae, or young, of various moths and beetles are feeding safely between the leaf's layers. Etchings in a tree's bark show where beetles have bored inside to feed on its wood while under cover.

Many insects even alter plants to create places to hide. Some caterpillars roll up leaves and seal them shut with sticky silk. Weaver ants seal leaves together with silk made by their larvae, which the adult ants use as if they were glue sticks. Some insects, including species of aphids, midges, and wasps, spur plants to grow protective cases. These cases, called galls, are hard knobs with spongy interiors. As larvae feed on the plant, their saliva induces the growth of these galls.

Larger animals also take advantage of the safe shelter provided by plants, rocks, and other parts of their habitat. Birds hide their nests amid grasses, tuck them among branches, bury them deep inside burrows, and conceal them in tree holes.

Staying hidden for many hours is not necessary for an animal that can get to a hiding place quickly. Many small rodents feed close to their burrows so they can dive into them at the first glimpse of a hawk overhead. Crabs scuttle swiftly beneath stones. The pancake tortoise of East Africa, which has a flat, flexible shell, wedges itself into a crevice between rocks. The turtle braces its legs so that it cannot easily be pulled out of its hiding spot. The chuckwalla, a lizard that lives in the southwestern United

HIDING BY DAY OR NIGHT

Many species make use of hideaways only when they are inactive. Raccoons, for example, are largely nocturnal—they are most active at night. During most daylight hours, they are curled up in a tree cavity, a woodpile, or even an attic, fast asleep. At night, they emerge to look for food. Their meals often include other nocturnal animals, such as slugs or mice.

As a result of being nocturnal, an animal not only avoids predators that are active by day, but also avoids competing with animals that eat the same food. Two different species that both feed on insects, for example, can use the same resource without competing directly if one is part of the day crew and the other takes the night shift.

Of course, some predators also are active at night. A nocturnal moth, for example, may be caught by a bat. The bat, in turn, may be caught by an owl.

States, also darts into crevices. Then, it inflates its lungs with air so that its body swells up, wedging it in place.

A LIFE IN HIDING

A variety of species go to the extreme: They spend most of their lives in hiding. Over millions of years, they have adapted to surviving in habitats that keep them under cover.

Many kinds of clams, for example, burrow into sandy or muddy beaches. Some species live just under the surface, while others dig deeply. A large clam called the geoduck can bury itself 3 feet (1 meter) below the surface.

By burrowing, a clam protects itself from being washed away by waves, drying out in the sun, and being an easy target for predators. It does not need to leave its hiding place to find food. Instead, the clam opens its paired shells and reaches up through the sand with a body part called a siphon. The <u>siphon</u> takes in water, which the clam filters to extract particles of food.

If the clam senses vibrations rippling through the sand, it quickly pulls in its siphon. Vibrations may mean a predator is investigating its hiding spot. The clam also may burrow more deeply to escape. Some clams can dig quickly: The razor clam can move 9 inches (22 centimeters) in 1 minute.

Other animals find safety in living underground, too. Earthworms spend much of the day burrowing through the soil. If caught by a bird's <u>probing</u> beak, an earthworm struggles to resist being yanked out of the ground. It grabs onto the walls of its burrow with <u>bristles</u> that line its sides. The worm's hind end also bulges to help clamp it in place.

A mole digging through the earth can send earthworms <u>scuttling</u> out of the soil. Moles eat earthworms and even store them for later, biting them and then stuffing them into holes in their tunnels. A mole rarely needs to poke its head above ground; there, an owl, fox, or weasel might pounce on it.

STAYING STILL

A prey animal that senses danger does not always seek a hiding place. Some species first try another way of avoiding detection: freezing in place. Many predators can easily spot prey in motion, but are less likely to notice a still animal, especially if it blends into the background.

A moving rabbit out in the open, for example, is an easy target for a hawk. To avoid being spotted, the rabbit crouches low and freezes in place. Its stillness reduces the chances of it being seen, and its low profile makes it look more like a mound of dirt than a round-bodied animal sitting on the ground.

ESCAPE HATCHES

Animals dig dwellings underground for many reasons. A den or burrow provides relief from extreme heat or cold. It can serve as a nursery for helpless young. Some animals store food in their burrows. A handy burrow also provides a safe spot when a predator appears.

Prairie dogs, which live on the grasslands of the United States, build extensive communities of burrows called towns. At the sight of a predator, a prairie dog immediately alerts its family and neighbors with shrill barks. In a flash, the prairie dogs dive into their burrows and out of sight. Their tunnels, which spread far, wide, and deep, provide the animals with many hideouts and escape routes.

Diggers, such as chipmunks and ground squirrels, also include emergency exits in their homes. That way, there's an escape route if a badger digs up the burrow or a snake slips into it. African mammals called meerkats have hundreds of tunnels called "bolt holes" in their territory. If a predator appears, they run, or "bolt," into them.

Ground squirrels, like this marmot, create dwellings underground in part to hide quickly from predators.

In much the same way, newborn deer lie still among ferns and grasses while their mothers spend time away from them, feeding on leaves. The fawns, born without any odor that would lure a predator, rely on their stillness as well as their spots to avoid detection on the sun-dappled woodland floor. Pronghorn antelope fawns remain still for hours on end, lying in tall grass to escape the notice of coyotes and eagles. The chicks of spotted sandpipers and many other birds also crouch and freeze when danger threatens.

Though many crouch-and-freeze creatures also benefit from coloration that helps them blend in with their background, such camouflage is not a requirement for "the freeze" to work. A squirrel, for example, is usually a highly visible animal as it busily dashes along branches or springs across a lawn. Should a dog or other animal threaten it, however, the squirrel scrambles up a tree trunk, circles to the side of the trunk opposite the predator, and freezes. If the predator follows it, the squirrel scurries to the other side of the trunk and freezes again. Using this spiraling method, the squirrel keeps a blockade between it and its attacker—even if the attacker is incapable of climbing the tree in pursuit.

HIDING IN PLAIN SIGHT

Camouflage, also known as cryptic coloration, is the one-size-fits-all defense in the world of animals. Animals as small as insects and as large as the boldly patterned giraffe—towering at a height of 18 feet (6 m)—depend on their cryptic colorations to help them blend in.

Colors and patterns may camouflage an animal not only by helping it blend in, but also by breaking up its shape. That way, a predator does not recognize it at first. An animal's coloring can

Walkingsticks are insects that look like twigs. They are able to blend in with trees to avoid predators.

hide the roundness of its body, making it look flat. Colors and patterns also can help hide an animal's shadow.

Cryptic coloration can be as simple as the sandy fur of a fennec fox, which blends with the tones of its desert home. It can be as complex as the camouflage of a giant swallowtail caterpillar, which looks like a bird dropping on a leaf. The fox "hides in plain sight," while the caterpillar stays safe by resembling something that does not interest a predator one bit.

Many cryptically colored animals just need to freeze or lie low to be protected. A pointy thorn bug sitting on a stem, for example, looks like a thorn. A grasshopper or katydid that resembles a leaf just needs to sit on a leafy twig to blend in and look like a leaf.

Some animals go one step further and behave in ways that enhance their camouflage.

Walkingsticks are part of this cast of animal actors. These long, thin insects naturally resemble twigs, complete with sharply bent limbs and bumpy joints. They are closely related to the fantastically shaped leaf insects, which have body parts shaped and colored to look like leaves—right down to leaf veins, nibbled edges, and brown spots of decay. But walkingsticks don't just look like sticks, and leaf insects don't just look like leaves. They act like them, too. While sitting still they sway slowly, mimicking the motion of a twig or leaf in the breeze.

Leaf insects have been known to dangle from a stem by one leg, as if they were leaves about to drop. If threatened, many leaf insects will fall to the ground, landing on their feet and scuttling away.

Other insects imitate plant galls, seeds, and flowers. The African flower mantis takes on the coloring of the flower on which it lives. This is also true of the Malaysian orchid mantis, which has legs that look like flower petals. The camouflage patterns on many moths' wings imitate patterns of tree bark and the lichen growing on it.

Moths instinctively use this camouflage to their advantage. The pine hawk-moth perches on a tree with its head pointing up. This lines up the stripes on its wings with the bark's furrows. The waved umber moth perches sideways on trees. That's because its stripes run across its wings. The sideways perch lines up these stripes with the bark's pattern.

Among the insects, caterpillars excel at combining cryptic coloration with deceptive behavior. A caterpillar's job is to eat and grow while avoiding being eaten by birds. A caterpillar must also avoid tiny wasps eager to lay their eggs on it. The eggs hatch into larvae that feed on the caterpillar.

A Costa Rican rainforest species of moth caterpillar called *Navarcostes limnatis* looks like a diseased leaf covered with fungus. It adds a rocking motion to this disguise so that it appears to be quivering in a breeze. Another caterpillar, the larva of a butterfly called the meander leafwing, crawls to the tip of a leaf after hatching. It eats the parts of the leaf that stick out on either side of the sturdy rib running down the leaf's middle. Then it sits on the rib so that it looks like a bit of nibbled leaf itself. The caterpillar will continue to eat the leaf over the next few days. It binds scraps of leaf to the rib with silk secreted by its body and hides among them.

Insects are stars when it comes to combining camouflage with a convincing performance, but other animals also use this tactic. The leafy sea dragon of Australian waters is one example. It has frills that make it look like a bit of drifting seaweed. The sea dragon also rocks slowly and rhythmically, mirroring the swaying of seaweed in its habitat.

Half a world away, the leaf fish of South America's Amazon River floats slowly on its side, its flattened, brown body resembling a dead leaf drifting in the water. Its snout looks like the leaf's stalk. This behavior allows the fish to avoid predators and hunt its own prey without being noticed.

Many tree frogs also imitate leaves or other plant parts. The red-eyed tree frog, for example, snuggles into the curve of a leaf during the day. Its bright green body blends with the leaf. The frog tucks its legs and big orange feet close to its blue-and-yellow sides so that the vivid colors are hidden. Finally, it closes its bulging red eyes, hiding them under gold-flecked lids. The frog can see through these lids to watch for danger as it naps.

Even some larger animals manage to pull off the trick of resembling an object. The potoo, a nocturnal bird of Central and South America, spends the day perched on a dead branch. Its feathers, mottled with brown and gray, work as camouflage.

The potoo holds its body at an angle that makes it look like just another dead branch. On the other side of the globe, a look-alike nocturnal bird called the tawny frogmouth poses the same way.

Another bird actor is the American bittern, which lives in wetlands. When it is startled, it stretches its long, thin neck and body and points its sharp bill to the sky. In this position, the streaks of brown running down its breast blend in with the tall, grassy plants around it. The bittern also sways gently, just like the breeze-ruffled reeds.

CHANGING COLOR

Sometimes, an animal's camouflage won't work if the habitat changes or an animal travels to another part of its habitat. A number of animals solve this problem by changing color.

Some animals change color as the seasons change. The willow ptarmigan, an Arctic bird, is mottled brown in summer and blends in with the ground, rocks, and plants. In winter, it is white with a black tail and nearly disappears against a background of snow and occasional twigs. In spring and fall, as it molts (sheds) old feathers and grows new ones, the bird is a mixture of brown and white—just like the patchy snow-spotted world around it.

Some animals change color within weeks or days. Many caterpillars change color as they grow, shedding a skin of one color to reveal another that can protect them better as they move about more to feed. Crab spiders can change color in just a few days to match the flowers in which they lurk. Bark bugs of Central America grow darker when moistened with water. This helps them blend in with rain-darkened tree trunks.

Some reptiles, fish, and other creatures can change color in just a few hours. Many tree frogs, for example, can go from green to brown. Horned lizards of the southwestern United States can

The feathers of the willow ptarmigan change color with the seasons: white in winter months to blend with snow and brown or mixed colors in other months to blend with plants and the earth. This enables the bird to often be naturally camouflaged from predators.

change their brown and gray tones to best fit their surroundings. The flounder, a flat-bodied fish with its eyes on the side of its head, lies on the ocean floor and takes on the color and texture of the sandy, stony surface in as little as two hours.

Other animals work even faster. Many octopuses, cuttlefish, and squids can change color in less than one second. An octopus can change from solid red to multiple colors, or even white, to match its background. It can also change the texture of its skin to resemble sand or stones. A cuttlefish can make light and dark waves ripple down its back, reflecting the way sunlight shimmers in water.

MASKING: ANIMALS IN DISGUISE

Some species push the defense tactics of hiding and camouflage to the max by actually wearing costumes. This behavior is known as **masking**.

The decorator crab, found in the eastern Pacific Ocean, is named for its habit of disguising itself. The crab picks seaweed, anemones, and sponges and puts them on its shell. Bristles on the shell work like Velcro to hold these items in place. In this disguise, the crab looks like another weed-covered rock. When the crab outgrows its shell and sheds it during molting, it takes the decorations off its old shell and plants them on its new one.

Decorator crabs share the eastern Pacific with sharp-nosed crabs, which sometimes stick seaweed on the sharp front edges of their shells. Other species of crab disguise themselves, too. The camouflage crab of New Zealand adorns its shell and legs with seaweed (and sometimes snacks on bits of it). The sponge crab uses its hind legs to hold a live sponge on its shell. The shell is covered with algae, which has settled on the shell just as it would on a stone.

Hermit crabs sometimes plant anemones on their shells. Anemones have stinging cells in their tentacles, so they provide an extra layer of protection for the crab. In return, the crab takes them to new feeding grounds, and the anemones can dine on tidbits from the crab's meals. Another species, the anemone crab, has claws equipped with hooks for gripping anemones. Any predator that approaches this crab will have the stinging anemones waved in its face.

Some insects also use masking. A wavy-lined emerald caterpillar cuts petals from the flowers it feeds on. Then it attaches the petals to spines on its body and fastens them in place with silk. When the petals wilt, it replaces them. This habit has earned the caterpillar the alternative name of camouflaged looper. Other kinds of looper caterpillars mask themselves with flowers, leaves, and bits of bark.

The larvae of many kinds of caddis fly mask themselves in camouflaged cases. The cases are made out of material from the larva's freshwater habitat: grains of sand, small stones and shells, leaves, twigs, bits of wood, or pine needles. The materials are bound together with sticky or silky fluids produced by the larva's body. A hooked pair of legs at the larva's hind end hang on to the case as the larva creeps about in search of food.

Hiding, camouflage, and masking help animals avoid predators. Animals' behaviors and bodies have changed over millions of years in ways that help them survive. Scientists call these changes **adaptations**. The process of change over time is called **evolution**.

Predators have also evolved so that they could keep finding prey. When they do, the prey must turn to another form of self-defense.

2

Escape Artists

HIDING, STANDING STILL, and camouflage help many animals avoid predators, but these defenses do not work all the time. Predators may find hiding places, stumble over prey lying stock-still, or discover that a leaf is actually an insect in disguise. Prey animals need a second line of defense.

For many animals, this defense is escape. Escape often means fleeing as quickly as possible. Escape also may involve behaviors that buy an animal a few extra seconds to get away. This could be startling a predator or distracting it. Some animals go so far as to actually lose body parts to aid in their escape. A few appear to give up by playing dead.

FLEEING

An animal without a burrow or other hiding place can choose between fight and flight. It can stand its ground and face a predator or make a quick getaway. Fighting may be used as a last resort; fleeing is the first response to danger.

Many long-legged, hoofed animals literally run for their lives, relying on sheer speed to escape. Horses, for example, can gallop at speeds of 30 miles (48 kilometers) per hour or more.

Deer race away just as quickly. The pronghorn of western North American grasslands can run about 50 miles (80 km) per hour.

This burst of speed may enable an animal to leave its pursuer in the dust. If the predator persists, however, many hoofed animals can run fast for several miles. A pronghorn can run at 35 miles (56 km) per hour for about 4 miles (6 km).

Running works well for speedy four-legged animals. It also serves some two-legged ones. The ostrich, the world's largest bird at 8 feet tall (2.4 m), cannot fly. Other than lions and jackals, few animals prey on it. If pursued, an ostrich can outrun and outlast most predators. It can cruise at speeds up to 40 miles (64 km) an hour and run at a slightly slower speed for 20 minutes or

When fleeing a predator, the basilisk lizard musters up enough energy to be able to run on water.

more. The rhea, a flightless bird of South America, can also run swiftly and turn on a dime. Roadrunners of the southwestern United States deserts can fly, but prefer to run. They can zip along at 18.6 miles (30 km) an hour.

The basilisk lizard normally gets around on four legs, but switches to two when it's threatened. The lizard lives in trees in rainforests of Central America. When a predator creeps up on it, the basilisk drops out of the tree and lands in the water. Then, it rises on its hind legs and runs across the surface of the water. The basilisk dashes about 15 feet (4.5 m) in three seconds flat before dropping forward to swim with all four legs.

A kangaroo cannot run, but it can leap away from danger. A red kangaroo can hop at 20 miles (32 km) an hour for long distances, and 30 miles (48 km) an hour for a short distance. Some people have clocked red kangaroos going even faster. Grasshoppers and crickets leap to safety, too. Beach hoppers, which are related to pill bugs, pop into the air by snapping their abdomens and pushing with four of their hind legs.

Swimming, slithering, climbing, and flying from danger all work just as well as running and jumping. An octopus, for example, escapes predators by filling its body with water, then pushing the water out through a tube-like body part called a siphon. This motion, called jetting, lets an octopus scoot away quickly in any direction. As it jets away, it emits a cloud of ink to hide its escape and further confuse its pursuer. Shellfish called scallops also jet away from danger. When a scallop senses that a sea star is near, it opens and shuts its shell, forcing out jets of water that scoot it away.

Another ocean creature, the flying fish, escapes predators by swimming quickly just under the water's surface, then streaking up and out of the water while stretching out a pair of wing-like fins. It sails through the air for up to 20 seconds before diving back into the water.

Some animals roll away from danger. Wheel spiders, which live in Africa's Namib Desert, start their escape from predatory wasps by running. Then, they suddenly fold their legs and flip sideways to roll down sand dunes like wheels. They can roll at a speed of about 3 feet (1 m) per second. The caterpillar of the mother-of-pearl moth also goes for a spin to escape by curling into a circle and then pushing off. A species of mantis shrimp, found along some Pacific shores, rolls up and pushes itself along in a series of backward somersaults.

Many predators, however, also have speed on their side. Their prey must often use other tactics besides pure speed to make their escape.

One way to make a pursuer work harder is to zigzag. A rabbit running from a coyote, for example, does not run endlessly in a straight line. Instead, it dodges back and forth, forcing the coyote to change direction and make sharp turns, too. Zigzagging is easier for a rabbit, which is small, than for the larger coyote. The coyote also cannot tell when the rabbit will dodge this way or that, so it cannot plan its next move. In this way, the rabbit makes the chase more difficult and tiring for the coyote. Though a coyote may still succeed in catching its prey, there is a chance that it may tire out, give up, and go look for an easier meal.

Other animals also dart and dash when chased. A herd of impala, slender antelopes of African grasslands, not only run from a predator but also zigzag in all directions. Impala also leap over each other as they run, sometimes springing as high as 10 feet (3 m) into the air. This explosion of activity startles and confuses a predator. It also makes it difficult for a predator to chase any one animal.

Zigzagging mixed with freezing can confuse predators, too. Frogs and grasshoppers will jump in one direction, then freeze, only to pop off in another direction if the predator comes near. A predator may not be able to focus on its prey with all the unexpected starts and stops. Likewise, a cottontail rabbit may go from zigzagging to freezing as it flees. When it runs, it flashes its puffy white tail like a target. When it freezes, it sits on its tail. The predator may lose track of the rabbit because the tail has vanished.

STARTLING A PREDATOR

Anyone who has jumped when startled knows how a predator might feel when its prey suddenly bursts into motion after being nearly invisible. The shock of the prey's sudden reappearance is

ELUDING BATS

Bats hunt on the wing at night. They send out pulses of sound and listen for the echoes to locate their prey. This process is called echolocation. Using it, a bat can pinpoint even tiny insects in flight.

Insects have developed escape behaviors to avoid echolocation. Some moths can hear the high-pitched sounds that bats send out. A moth may fly in loops to avoid being detected. If a moth senses that a bat is close, it will simply fold its wings and drop from the sky.

Some moths go one step further and jam the bat's signals. A moth does this by making sounds that are similar to the echoes that the bat is trying to hear. This can throw the bat off course just long enough to help the moth escape.

Scientists have recently discovered that some moths make sounds that warn bats not to eat them because they taste bad. Bats quickly learn to avoid these moths after a few taste tests. Some species of moth that do not taste bad imitate the sounds of the foul-tasting ones, which tricks the bats into steering clear of them, too.

enough to make a predator flinch or pause for a fraction of a second. That little bit of extra time can let an animal escape with its life.

A variety of animals even sport special colors or body parts to help them startle predators. These colors and parts are used in behaviors called **startle displays**. A startle display may be used to fend off an attack right from the start. Many startle displays of this type involve suddenly flashing a vivid color or pattern.

This is the tactic used by the io moth, which lives in North America. At rest, an io moth is pale yellow or brown. But if a bird attempts to grab it, the io moth quickly moves its forewings. This reveals two hind wings boldly colored with a pair of big black spots surrounded by a circle of yellow. These spots look like eyes, and are called **eyespots**. To a bird, the display of eyespots may look like the sudden appearance of a larger bird, such as an owl—its own predator. The startled bird may fly away rather than risk its life, or it may pause long enough for the moth to escape.

Eyespots are found on the wings of hundreds of species of moths and butterflies. They are also seen on many caterpillars. A swallowtail butterfly's plump green body has two huge yellow eyespots on its humped front end. This makes it look like a snake. When threatened, the vine hawk moth's brown caterpillar curls into a "C" and bulges its yellow eyespots. A Malaysian hawk moth caterpillar puffs up its front end when threatened. This makes its eyespots open wide. It also snaps its head back and forth as if it were a snake about to strike.

Other insects flash startling eyespots, too. The African flower mantis, which usually blends in with the shapes and colors of its flowery habitat, flares out wings with eyespots when it is threatened. The eyed click beetle has two black eyespots behind its head. An Australian moth caterpillar has eyespots that are normally hidden in the folds of its body. When it flexes its hind end, the folds open like lids to reveal the "eyes."

Patches of color that do not look like eyes also make effective startle displays. These colors are often hidden until an animal flees. The sudden appearance of this **flash coloration** can stop a predator in its tracks just long enough to let the prey escape.

A red-eyed tree frog, for example, usually blends in with the leaf on which it sleeps. If a predator bothers it, the frog first pops open its enormous red eyes. Then it leaps away, turning from a plain green frog into a rainbow of color as its orange-footed legs unfold and its blue and yellow sides appear. This sudden splash of color startles the predator and buys the frog time to get away.

Octopuses also abruptly give up on camouflage when they are under attack. An alarmed octopus can burst into startling colors or patterns in less than a second. A fish or turtle that sees

A flash of the red-eyed tree frog's large red eyes can surprise predators, and give it time to escape.

BLUFFING

Startle displays are often part of a behavior called bluffing. Bluffing is a tactic used by animals to make them "look tough" to a predator. An animal that may be completely harmless acts as if it is actually quite ferocious and possibly dangerous. A predator may back off rather than risk getting injured.

Many lizards combine a startle display with a bluff. A chameleon facing a predator, for example, may suddenly turn dark as it puffs up its body to look larger. It also hisses, often revealing a brightly colored mouth.

The frilled lizard of Australia confronts predators with a wide-open yellow or pink mouth. It adds to this display by opening huge flaps of skin on its neck, which are splotched with red, orange, black, and white. The big frills make the lizard look much larger and more intimidating. Another Australian lizard, the bearded dragon, likewise gapes its yellow-lined mouth and raises a beard of spiky skin under its chin. The beard also turns blue-black.

its intended meal suddenly turn black or zebra-striped is often scared away.

Many kinds of stick insects, grasshoppers, butterflies, moths, and other insects also flash bright colors when fleeing a predator. The colors disappear when they leap or fly to a new spot and fold their wings. They then blend in with their surroundings as they sit perfectly still.

Sometimes just a spot of color can do the trick. The shingleback skink of Australia is a stumpy, short-legged lizard. Its earth-tone colors usually hide it. However, the skink startles potential predators by suddenly opening its mouth and sticking out its thick, blue tongue. It also huffs and puffs, hissing like a snake. Another Australian lizard that uses this startle display is the blue-tongued skink, named for its turquoise tongue.

An Australian legless lizard called the excitable delma does not have startling colors, but it still spooks predators with its behavior. If bothered, this animal twists and turns its body violently as it slithers away. This odd behavior may startle and confuse a predator.

DEFLECTING AN ATTACK

Startle displays and bluffs can help an animal escape in the nick of time. Another tactic is to trick a predator into attacking the "wrong" part of its prey or misjudging which direction the prey will go as it tries to escape. An animal can live to see another day if it can keep its head and body safe by getting a predator to merely nip its tail instead.

Colors, markings, and behaviors that encourage a predator to focus on the wrong end of its prey are called **deflection displays** because they redirect, or deflect, an attack.

Deflection displays often make use of eyespots. Unlike eyespots that are flashed to scare a predator, these eyespots show on an animal's hind end at all times. They draw a predator's attention away from the prey's head. As a predator lunges, it focuses on the prominent eyespot at the prey's tail end instead of on the prey's head. The prey's actual eyes may be hidden among stripes or spots.

Eyespots like these are common among fish, especially coral-reef species such as butterfly fish. The four-eyed butterfly fish, for example, has false eyes near its tail that look just like its real eyes. The threadfin butterfly fish has a dark spot on a fin toward its rear. A dark stripe on its head runs through its actual eye, which make it less noticeable. Angled stripes on its sides also guide a predator's eye toward its tail. If attacked, each fish may lose a bit of its tail, but escape with its life.

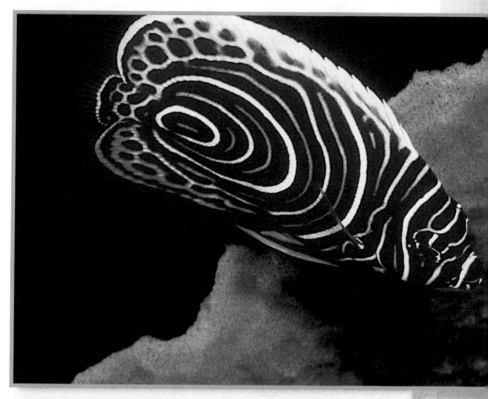

A juvenile emperor angelfish has an eyespot near its tail, which makes a predator focus on the wrong end.

Juvenile emperor angelfish, another coral-reef species, are covered with loops of white and light blue on a dark background. These loops swirl around a large eyespot near the angelfish's tail, while its actual eyes disappear among the stripes on its head. A predator's gaze is naturally pulled to the wrong end.

Insects also use eyespots in their deflection displays. These eyespots are always visible, not like the eyespots used to startle predators. They are also smaller and closer to the wings' edges.

Many species of butterflies sport such eyespots on their hind wings. A bird that snaps at the wrong end of such a butterfly leaves notches in the wings but loses out on a meal. Some butterflies have hind wings tipped with fake legs and antennae. Scientists have noticed that some of these butterflies will even creep backward along a stem for a second or two after landing, which might help fool a nearby predator. One butterfly found in Malaysia has such a convincing "head" on its hind end that it is sometimes called the back-to-front butterfly.

Other insects rely on false heads to dodge predators, too. A lanternfly of Southeast Asia has antennae lookalikes dangling from the ends of its wings near a pair of eyespots. When the wings are folded, the lanternfly's tail looks like a head. The insect even walks backward when it senses danger. Some lanternflies turn this trick around and have heads that look like tails.

The giant desert centipede of the southwestern United States is not an insect, but it uses the false-head trick, too. Its tail end looks just like its head, right down to antennae-like attachments. If a predator grabs the centipede's hind end because it mistakes it for the head, the centipede can twist around and bite it.

The shingleback skink, a lizard of Australia, also uses this tactic. Its stumpy head and tail look nearly identical. A predator that grabs the wrong "head" will be surprised to see the skink scurry off in the opposite direction.

Many snakes also use the two-headed trick. They roll up in a ball and hide their heads in their coils when under attack. Then they wave their tails to threaten the predator and deflect its attack. These snakes sometimes have bright colors on their tails that enhance this trick. Southeast Asian snakes called kraits, for example, wave red tails.

The ring-necked snake of North America coils its tail to display the bright orange-red underside. The color and coiling can distract a predator. In Africa, the shovel-snouted snake coils its tail, too. Other kinds of snakes even jab their tails at their attackers as if they were going to bite them.

Tail markings are common among animals, and some scientists are taking a second look at them to see which ones may be used as deflection displays. The black tip on a weasel's tail, for example, may help trick a hawk into trying to grab the skinny tail instead of the body or head.

LOSING LIMBS AND TAILS

Some animals whose tails are grabbed have a surprise in store for their attackers. Shockingly, their tails break off while their owners escape.

Many North American species of skinks, for example, have bright blue tails when they are young. A skink's blue tail works as a deflection display to protect its head. But if a predator actually seizes the tail, it breaks off. The skink runs away, leaving its tail wriggling and squirming behind it. The predator gets nothing but a bony mouthful. The skink's tail later grows back.

The broken-tail trick is used by many kinds of lizards, even ones that do not have brightly colored tails. Geckos, anoles, and iguanas all can shed their tails. This is also true of some legless lizards, which are called "glass snakes" because of the way their tails shatter when they break. The predator doesn't break these lizards' tails: The lizards do it themselves. The movement of muscles in the tail causes one of the tailbones to snap in half.

Some rodents can also shed part of their tails. Spiny rats, which live in parts of South and Central America, have tails that break off. Gerbils and some species of rats and mice lose the outer layer of skin and fur on their tails. The spiny rats are left with stumps, but rodents that shed their tails' covering lose the rest of the tail later. Unlike lizards, rodents do not grow back the missing parts.

Tails are not the only body parts shed by animals. Some animals dispose of their limbs instead. Some species of octopus can release some of their arms if they are attacked. The wriggling arms distract the predator and let the prey escape. Large tropical centipedes also toss off legs if they feel threatened. The lost legs writhe and even make squeaky noises to distract predators. Octopuses grow new limbs. Centipedes don't, but they have so many legs that the loss of a few doesn't harm them.

A crab also can drop a claw or leg if attacked. Some species pinch their attackers first and then release the pinched claw. The crab runs away while the predator frantically tries to remove the painful claw. Lobsters also release their claws in this way. Crabs and lobsters replace the claws over time as they molt and grow new outer coverings called **exoskeletons**.

Insects and spiders, such as the daddy longlegs, have legs that are easily pulled off by predators. They do not grow new legs, but get around just fine with the remaining ones.

Some geckos save their skins by losing them. These geckos are covered with an outer layer of skin that is only loosely connected to the skin underneath. The outer layer slips off if a predator grabs them. The gecko scurries away as if it had simply popped out of a sleeping bag.

Birds cannot shed their skins, but they can lose feathers. Normally, a bird's feathers cannot easily be pulled out. However, a predator that grabs a bird's tail is often left with a mouthful of feathers. This feather loss is called fright molting. Some scientists think it may help a bird wriggle out of the clutches of an owl or other predator, just as a butterfly sheds wing scales as it struggles to escape a spider's web. They also think that a bird can fright molt in midair, leaving a burst of feathers behind it that might deflect a hawk's attack.

Though many animals lose parts of their outsides to defend themselves, some species of sea cucumbers lose their insides instead. These plump, slippery ocean animals usually are protected by sticky mucus covering their bodies. If a sea cucumber is attacked, it expels its internal organs from its hind end. The sticky guts can trap a crab or startle a bigger predator. Then the sea cucumber creeps away while its attacker either struggles with the messy organs or eats them. Within a few weeks, the sea cucumber grows new organs.

PLAYING DEAD

A variety of animals escape death by playing dead. This defense is called death feigning. Animals that play dead may seem as if they are offering themselves up on a platter. Yet, many predators hunt prey in response to movement. Many animals also do not eat prey that they have not killed. By playing dead, an animal may make its attacker lose interest. A predator may also get careless if its prey seems to be dead. It may relax its grip and give the prey a chance to escape.

Many insects are known to feign death. These insect actors include many species of beetles, grasshoppers, stick insects, and caterpillars. Some insects curl up and remain still. Others let go of branches and drop to the ground. Certain reptiles, such as chameleons and many tree snakes, also drop to the ground and lie still.

Many birds also go limp when caught by a predator, and then instantly "come back to life" at the first chance for escape. Baby ospreys play dead in the nest when their mother gives a warning call.

Going limp and lying still works well for many animals, but a few species deserve Academy Awards for their death-feigning skills. Among these "best actors" are the opossum and the hognose snake, both found in North America.

An opossum defends itself at first by growling, hissing, and showing its teeth. If this does not frighten away the dog or other

The opossum keeps predators away by curling up and playing dead. This pretend act is the reason for the phrase "playing possum," which means to fake being dead.

SEA SLUGS VERSUS SPINY LOBSTER

Octopuses, squids, and cuttlefish squirt ink as they escape. Scientists assumed this was a defense behavior. Now, because of a recent discovery in sea slugs, researchers are taking a closer look at the ink.

Certain species of sea slugs also produce inky clouds. The ink was known to taste bad. Now, however, scientists know that the ink changes the behavior of a predator called the spiny lobster. Chemicals in the ink seem to muddle the lobster's actions. An "inked" lobster gives up its attack on a slug. It may groom itself and begin digging and grabbing at the sand with its claws, as if it were feeding. Perhaps other animals' ink also affects their predators in ways yet to be discovered.

animal that is threatening it, the opossum "drops dead." It rolls onto its side, rounds its back, and goes limp. Its tongue lolls from its open mouth. Its eyes close halfway—just enough to let it keep track of its predator. An opossum will keep playing dead even if the predator bites it. It does not revive until the predator goes away and the coast is clear again.

Hognose snakes also use other defenses before resorting to playing dead. A frightened hognose snake will first raise its head, spread its neck wide, and hiss. Then, it will produce a bad smell. If this act fails, the snake flips onto its back and lies still. Like the opossum, it opens its mouth and lets its tongue hang out. If it is picked up and placed on its belly, it will keep flipping onto its back and playing dead.

3

Animal Armor

A GIANT REPTILE lumbers through a patch of low-growing plants. It swings its head to the side to snatch a mouthful of leaves. The head is covered with flat, bony plates. Sharp triangles stick out from the sides like horns. Spikes also run down the sides of its broad, domed back, which is shingled with bony plates.

This spiky, armored reptile is an ankylosaurus, a dinosaur that lived about 70 million years ago. It was one of the most heavily armored of all dinosaurs. The bony plates in its skin were welded to its skeleton in some places. Even its eyelids contained pads of bone.

Few meat-eating dinosaurs could take on this armored dinosaur, which was as long as a school bus and as heavy as a tank. If a predator did try to sink its teeth into an ankylosaurus's armored back, the reptile had one more defense. It swung its huge tail at its enemy—a tail that ended in a massive club of fused bone.

Armor was a primary form of defense for prehistoric animals. Today, many animals still use it. Sharp spikes and spines, tough bony plates, shells, and thick skin help protect animals from the teeth, jaws, and claws of predators.

SPIKES AND SPINES

Most insects have thick outer skeletons that serve as armor. These exoskeletons may also boast spikes and spines, which add to an insect's defense. Many species of crickets and grasshoppers, for example, have spines on their legs and backs. Many ants have spines in the middle of their back that protect them from other insects' nipping jaws. Praying mantises have spurs on their claws that not only help in grabbing prey, but also inflict wounds on predators.

Caterpillars typically have soft bodies. This makes them tempting morsels for predators. But most caterpillars have other ways to protect themselves. Some have spikes or spiny, hair-like

A caterpillar's bristles, like those of this gypsy moth caterpillar, can be used as a defense against predators.

bristles. Caterpillars can be so bristly that they appear to have fur. The bristles irritate a predator's skin and eyes. If a predator accidentally inhales some bristles, they can hurt its nose, throat, and lungs.

Other small animals have spines, spikes, and bristles, too. The spined spider has an array of big, red spines on its body. Millipedes have bundles of barbed bristles along their bodies and on their hind ends. These bristles come off and get stuck in the faces and jaws of ants and other predators.

Large spiders called tarantulas also defend themselves with bristles. A tarantula uses two of its hind legs to rub bristles off its abdomen, which sends hundreds of the tiny barbed bristles at the attacker. The bristles irritate its eyes, nose, and mouth.

Spikes and spines also protect animals that live underwater. The tiny young, or larvae, of crabs have spines that help them float while also repelling fish. Likewise, spiny lobsters are protected by spines that line their antennae and point forward along their shells. The crown-of-thorns sea star is also spiny. This sea star has as many as 19 arms, with sturdy pink or yellow spines poking out of its orange, red, and purple skin. The spines not only pierce skin, but also deliver a dose of painful **venom**.

Sea urchins are like living pincushions. Their hard, round bodies bristle with spines. An urchin uses its spines to help it move. The sharp spines also keep many predators at bay. Some sea urchins' spines are connected to glands that make venom. Long-spined hatpin urchins have venomous spines that can be up to 12 inches (30 cm) long. Some species of fish and jellyfish hide in hatpin urchins.

Stonefish have spines connected to venom glands, too. These are well-camouflaged fish that lie on the seabed in some tropical waters. Their spines pierce and kill predators that grab them. Surgeonfish, which also live in tropical waters, have a pair of

Sea urchins, like this common sea urchin found along the coast of Scotland, use their bristles for moving as well as defense.

razor-like spines on either side of the tail. The fish slashes at attackers with these spines.

Sticklebacks are named for the spines that stick up on their backs. A stickleback can lock these spines in an upright position. The number of spines varies, as shown by their names, which range from three- to fifteen-spined stickleback.

The porcupine fish's name is likewise a clue to its defense. This fish is covered with sharp spines. When threatened, the fish inflates its body with water, and the spines stick out in all directions. This makes the fish too big for some predators to swallow. It startles other predators, which may decide not to tackle the suddenly enlarged prey.

A variety of lizards also wear spike-studded armor. The well-named thorny devil resembles a miniature dragon as it strolls across the Australian sand, looking for ants to eat. Spikes of many sizes jut from its legs, sides, tail, back, and head. Despite its name, a thorny lizard is not aggressive. If threatened, it tucks its head between its front legs. This makes a large, spiky bump on its neck stick out—a bump that looks like an even more unappetizing head than the lizard's actual one.

Just as prickly are the horned lizards of dry lands and deserts in parts of Mexico and the southwestern United States. A

This thorny devil shows off its spikes of many sizes as it walks along a street in the Northern Territory, Australia.

horned lizard has spines running down its sides, back, and tail. Strong, sharp horns jut from its head, making it look like a tiny triceratops. If a predator threatens it, a horned lizard puffs up its body so that its spines stick out. It also turns its head to present its horns. Some species can also squirt blood from the corners of their eyes. The blood can shoot out up to 3 feet (1 m). The blood tastes bad, so the squirt both surprises and disgusts a predator.

The armadillo lizard of southern Africa is also spiky. It makes the most of its spikes by rolling into a ball and grabbing its tail in its mouth when threatened. This turns the lizard into a prickly doughnut.

Mammals also make use of spines for protection. Porcupines, for example, fend off predators with spines called quills. There are about 25 species of porcupine. About half of them are found in Europe, Asia, and Africa. The rest are found in Central and South America, with one species living in North America.

A North American porcupine is covered with about 30,000 long, sharp quills. The quills range from half an inch (1.3 cm) to 5 inches (12.7 cm) long. A porcupine warns enemies before they attack. It lowers its head, lifts its tail, and raises its quills and rattles them. It also clacks its teeth, stamps its feet, and gives off a very strong smell from a patch of skin on its back.

If the attacker persists, the porcupine will back up toward it and whack it with its tail. The quills, which are barbed at the end, pop off the porcupine and stick in the attacker's skin. They are painful and can actually drill deeper into skin and muscles over time.

The African crested porcupine also warns predators not to mess with it. It shakes its tail, making a loud rattling noise with a clump of special, hollow quills. This porcupine also raises quills on its back that can be up to 20 inches (50 cm) long and are boldly striped in black and white. As a last resort, it will run sideways or backward to jab its quills into its foe.

A young lion tries to flip over an African crested porcupine in order to kill it in South Africa, where porcupines are the principal diet of Kalahari lions.

Hedgehogs are also prickly. A European hedgehog has about 5,000 short, sharp spines. Unlike a porcupine's quills, hedgehog spines do not come out of the skin when used for jabbing.

A hedgehog usually flees or hides in the face of danger. If it is cornered, it raises its spines and then rolls into a ball, protecting its soft belly and its head. A hedgehog can stay rolled up for many hours, and a predator is likely to give up prodding the unresponsive, prickly ball. An uncurled hedgehog, however, may leap backward into a predator or thrust its spiny body into its face.

Spines also protect spiny anteaters called echidnas. Echidnas are Australian monotremes (egg-laying mammals) that eat insects, snaring them with their long, sticky tongues. Hundreds of spines cover an echidna's body. A spine can be about 2 inches (60 mm) long. If threatened, an echidna digs quickly into the ground, leaving only its spiny back showing. It can also roll up into a ball or wedge itself into a crevice among rocks.

ARMORED ON THE INSIDE

Some animals have spikes that come into play only when they are attacked. Among these unusual animals is a mammal called the potto.

The potto is a slow-moving, tree-dwelling African animal. Three bones in its neck end in thick spines that stick up through the skin. The spines usually are buried in its thick fur. However, if threatened, a potto curls up so that its neck bends and the spines stick up. Some scientists have recently found that the spines are sensitive to touch and that pottos sometimes rub necks with each other. They are researching to see if pottos use their spines to communicate with one another.

A salamander called the sharp-ribbed newt also has hidden spines. Its spines are the ends of its ribs. If attacked, the newt pushes its ribs so that they form rows of bumps on its back. There are poison glands on the bumps. The sharp rib tips may also poke out of the newt's skin.

The hero shrew of West Africa does not show its strength; its armor is completely hidden inside. This armor is its one-of-a-kind backbone. Each bone in its spine has ridges on it and fits snugly into the bones on either side of it. The spine is also very flexible, and the ribs attached to it are very thick. A person weighing 160 pounds (72 kilograms) can stand on the shrew's back without harming it. Why the shrew's back is so strong is still a mystery, though its strength may certainly stop some predators' jaws from crushing it.

The army of spiny mammals includes the spiny rats of Central and South America. Some species of spiny rats have sturdy spines, while others have stiff, bristly hair. Spiny rats can also shed their tails to escape a predator's grip. Another group of spiny mammals, the tenrecs, is found on Madagascar, an island off the east coast of Africa. A tenrec can roll up into a ball like a hedgehog. It also has a powerful bite and will butt its enemy in the neck with its spiny head.

SHELLS

A sturdy shell is the primary defense for a variety of very slow-moving animals, such as turtles, tortoises, snails, and clams.

Turtles and tortoises are reptiles with bodies enclosed in shells. Turtles spend much or all of their lives in water, while tortoises live on land. Both have shells made of two parts: an upper section called the carapace and a lower section called the plastron.

The shell is basically a sturdy box made of bone. The inside of the carapace is made of bones fused together. These bones include the turtle's spine and ribs. The plastron is made of bone, too.

In most species, the outside of the carapace is covered with plates made of a tough material called keratin—the same substance that forms hooves and fingernails. These plates are called **scutes**. Some turtles have just a few scutes embedded in a thick skin on the carapace. Some have none at all.

Many turtles can pull their heads, tails, and legs partly or fully into their shells. Box turtles have hinged plastrons, so they can close the openings in their shells. Desert tortoises fold their thick, scaly legs in front of their withdrawn heads to form a shield. A turtle can stay inside its shell for hours, waiting for a predator to give up. It will stay tucked in while a predator sniffs it or rolls it around.

For slow-moving animals like the snail, a shell is a primary defense. This snail is resting on a leaf, but it can quickly disappear inside its shell if it senses a threat.

Snails, clams, mussels, and other mollusks also are protected by shells. The soft, boneless body of a mollusk is covered with a kind of skin called a mantle. In the mantle are glands that produce the materials that form the shell. These materials include minerals that the mollusk gets from its food and from the water, sand, or soil in which it lives.

A snail seems to carry its shell on its back, but much of its body is actually inside the shell. If threatened, the snail pulls its head and its muscular foot inside the shell. Many kinds of snails seal the shell's opening with a hard plate on the end of the foot. Sea snails called limpets have feet that work like suction cups and help them grip rocks firmly so that they are difficult to pry off.

INSECT ARMOR

Most insects' tough exoskeletons protect their bodies from predators and from drying out. However, some insects—including young insects, such as caterpillars—have soft bodies. They benefit by adding an extra layer of protective armor.

Scale insects, for example, are named for the armor they produce. A young scale insect finds a spot on a plant where it can feed. Then its body oozes substances that form a shield over it. The insect lives underneath this shield.

Different kinds of scale insects make different kinds of shields. Armored scale insects make hard, waxy shields. Soft scale insects make softer waxy coverings, or shields that look like balls of cotton. Ground pearls, which are related to scale insects, make round, waxy covers that look like beads.

Caterpillars of some moths make a sticky, bumpy covering for their bodies. Ants that bite these caterpillars end up with jaws full of goo. The ants' bodies and legs also become coated with the slime. The ants must work hard to scrape off the sticky material, which keeps them too busy to try to attack again.

Clams, oysters, and mussels are all bivalves: mollusks with two-part shells. A bivalve has a hinge between the halves of its shell. Depending on the species, it can partly or fully close its shell around its body. Many bivalves burrow deeply in sand or mud to stay hidden from predators, such as seabirds.

Mollusks called chitons have shells made of eight plates. A chiton clings to a rock with its wide, flat foot as it grazes on algae. It hangs on tightly enough to prevent being washed away by waves. If a predator manages to pull it off the rock, the chiton rolls up into an armor-plated ball.

In recent years, researchers discovered a snail living on the deep-sea floor that actually wears metal armor. This snail has not only a protective shell, but also extra-tough skin. Scales made of minerals, including iron, cover its soft body.

SCALES, SCUTES, AND SKIN

Tough skin and scales may be unusual in snails. However, they are typical armor for many other animals.

Armadillos, for example, are armor-plated mammals that live in Central and South America, as well as in parts of the southern

With the exception of its ears and belly, the nine-banded armadillo is completely covered by a bony armor. It can, however, tuck its limbs and head into its armor and huddle close to the ground to protect its belly.

United States. Their name, which means "little armored one" in Spanish, refers to their bony armor. Scientists call the armadillo's armor a carapace.

The carapace is made up of bony plates arranged in bands around the armadillo's body. The plates are covered by tough skin. Each bony band is separated from the ones next to it by a band of skin, allowing the armadillo to flex its body. The armadillo found in the United States is called the nine-banded armadillo. Its armor covers its head, body, legs, and tail. Only its belly and ears are unprotected.

If a coyote or other predator threatens it, a nine-banded armadillo's first defense is to flee. It zigzags as it runs away. If it cannot run away, it digs with its strong claws. It burrows into the ground in less than two minutes. The predator may pull on the armadillo's tail to yank it out of the burrow. This won't work because the armadillo hangs on with its claws. Its bony bands also help wedge it in place.

A nine-banded armadillo can also hunker down so that its carapace touches the ground. Then it can pull in its nose and feet. Playing dead or leaping abruptly into the air are other defenses. It can also curl its body slightly so that its nose and tail touch, though it cannot roll up into a ball.

The nine-banded armadillo is about the size of a cat. The pink fairy armadillo is much smaller—about as long as a dollar bill—but it is also a mighty digger. Like its larger cousin, it can swiftly dig a burrow when danger threatens. It runs into the burrow head first and plugs the opening with a plate of armor that covers its hind end.

The three-banded armadillo is the only armadillo that can roll itself up so tightly that it looks like a scaly croquet ball. This armadillo can also unroll slightly to peek out and see if its attacker is still there. If the attacker comes close to investigate, the

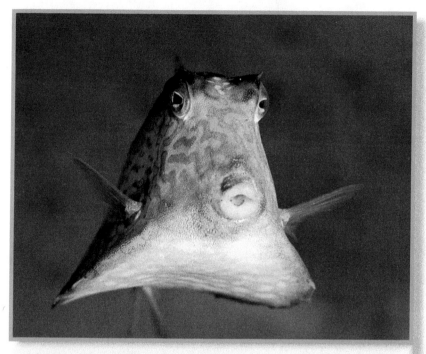

Only the tail, fins, eyes, and mouth stick out of a boxfish's boxy suit of armor, which is created by linked scales.

armadillo quickly slams its carapace shut again—an action that sometimes nips the attacker's nose.

In parts of Africa and Asia, scaly mammals called pangolins rely on protective body armor for defense, too. A pangolin is a long-tailed, ant-eating, nocturnal animal covered in a heavy coat of thick, overlapping scales. Only its belly and part of its face are exposed.

Unlike armadillos, all species of pangolin are able to roll into a tight ball. The scales also stand on edge so that they resemble spikes. If a predator pokes its nose between the scales, the pangolin can move so that the sharp scales pinch. All the while, glands under the pangolin's tail produce a bad-smelling fluid.

Animal armor also includes the bony scales of fish. Fish scales overlap to form a flexible but strong covering. The squared-off bodies of boxfish have scales that link together to make a boxy suit of armor. A boxfish's tail, fins, eyes, and mouth stick out of the box.

Sharks have skin covered with tiny, sharp teeth called "skin teeth" or dermal denticles. The denticles make the skin as rough as sandpaper. A shark's skin is like a strong but flexible suit of **chain mail**. A great white shark's skin is so dense with denticles that it even helps protect it from the bites of other sharks.

Crocodiles and alligators also have armor-like skin. Like other reptiles, they have tough, horn-like scales in their skin. Unlike most other reptiles, they also have strong bony plates embedded in the skin.

A rhinoceros does not have scales, but it does have thick skin. A rhino's skin ranges from about three-quarters of an inch (18 mm) deep in some places to nearly 2 inches (45 mm) on its shoulders. This helps protect a rhino from a predator's fangs and claws. The rhino also has a formidable horn. The only rhino likely to be attacked by a predator is an unguarded calf.

PENETRATING THE ARMOR

As populations of animals change over time, they develop defenses. Predator populations also evolve, developing body parts and behaviors that help them defeat their prey's defenses. Often this simply involves big teeth and strong jaws. A shark or crocodile, for example, can easily crunch through a turtle's shell. Sometimes, however, special behaviors are involved.

The bearded vulture, for example, knows how to open turtles' shells. This vulture is found in parts of Europe and Asia. It mainly feeds on animal bones left over from other animals' kills. To get at the food left inside a bone, the vulture carries the bone

ROLLING UP AS A DEFENSE

Three-banded armadillos and pangolins are not the only armored animals that roll up in the face of danger. Small, armadillo-like invertebrates called pill bugs roll up, too. Pill bugs are crustaceans, a group of animals that includes shrimp, crabs, and lobsters. The word *crustacean* comes from a Latin word meaning "crust" or "shell." It refers to the hard exoskeletons of these animals.

A pill bug can roll up so tightly that it looks like a small gray pea. Sowbugs are related to pill bugs, but cannot roll up. They must scurry away to escape predators such as spiders and centipedes. Pill millipedes and some kinds of cockroaches also can roll up when in danger.

Many snakes also curl up in a ball when threatened. One group of snakes, the ball pythons, is named for this behavior.

When in danger, pill bugs are able to use their segmented bodies to roll up into little pea-sized balls.

high into the air and drops it onto rocks to smash it apart. The vulture uses this same behavior to smash open a turtle's shell.

Gulls use this behavior, too. They carry clams and other shelled animals into the air, and then drop them onto rocks and roads. Crows likewise drop snails onto hard surfaces. Song thrushes hold snails in their beaks and bash them against favorite stones, which are known as thrush anvils.

A bird called the snail kite is named for its habit of eating almost nothing but apple snails. Its slim, hooked bill fits neatly into the spiral of an apple snail's shell. The bill's sharp tip snips a muscle in the snail, releasing the snail from its shell.

The oystercatcher, a bird that feeds on ocean shores, patrols shellfish beds to look for mussels or oysters with slightly opened shells. The bird stabs its long, sharp bill into one of these open shells, quickly cutting the muscles that clamp the shell closed. An oystercatcher may also open a shell by bashing at the hinge from the outside.

A sea snail gets past a clam's armor by using its raspy tongue to drill a hole in the shell. A sea star wraps its suckered arms around a clamshell and pulls. Eventually, the clam gets tired and the shell opens. Immediately, the sea star's stomach oozes out of its body and into the shell, where it digests the clam.

A sea star can even slip its stomach around a sea urchin's spines. A sunflower star is big enough to engulf a sea urchin and digest it, then "spit out" the shell and spines. A triggerfish also eats sea urchins. It flips them over, plucks off their spines, and then uses its strong teeth to bite through the shell.

Mammals have figured out ways to get around their prey's armor, too. A weasel-like animal called the fisher, for example, quickly flips over prickly porcupines so it can attack their soft undersides. Wolves, wolverines, and bobcats also prey on porcupines. A sea otter carries a stone underwater and uses it as a hammer to knock sea snails called abalone off rocks.

4

Bad Smells, Bad Tastes, and Powerful Poisons

HIDING, CAMOUFLAGE, AND ESCAPE help many animals stay out of the clutches of predators. Armor and other heavy-duty outsides help many animals survive being caught. A variety of animals use another weapon: chemicals that ward off predators or stop their attack after it has begun.

These chemicals may have a bad taste, a terrible smell, or both. They may irritate the skin as well as the senses. They also may be poisonous. Some can sicken a predator, or even kill it.

Chemical defenses are secret weapons, in one way, because they are contained inside the animals. But many animals do not try to keep them secret. These animals often are brightly colored, which helps warn predators that they are armed and dangerous. They may also behave in ways that announce their intention to use chemical defenses if pushed.

A chemical defense may be a primary defense: a defense that exists all the time, even when the animal is not in any danger. A poisonous insect, for example, is poisonous all the time.

A chemical defense can also be a secondary defense: a defense that is put to work after the animal has been threatened or attacked. A skunk, for example, doesn't always ooze bad-smelling fluid. First, it behaves in ways that warn the predator to go away. It will spray predators that do not heed the warning.

POISONOUS PREY

A poisonous animal has poison in its body. It does not typically have a special body part, such as a sting, for injecting the poison. Instead, a predator comes in contact with the poison when it seizes or eats the poisonous animal. Sometimes a predator learns its mistake while eating its prey—or even after it has swallowed it.

A bird that grabs the poisonous monarch butterfly will get a taste of the poison. This is often enough to make the bird drop the monarch. The bird learns that a monarch is an unpleasant meal, and the monarch escapes.

If the bird swallows the monarch, it regrets it. The monarch's poison does not kill the bird, but it does make the bird feel sick and throw up. Most birds remember this lesson for a long time and do not attempt to catch monarchs again. Scientists have found that the mere sight of a monarch can cause these "educated" birds to gag and retch, as if they were about to be sick.

Many poisonous animals produce foul fluids that cling to the predator or entrap it. The pill millipede, for example, oozes sticky droplets when it is attacked. The droplets stick to predators such as ants. As the ants frantically try to clean off the fluid, they gum themselves up even more. Meanwhile, the millipede escapes. A spider that eats a pill millipede will be paralyzed for several days. The poison even can affect birds and mice.

Some animals' poison can kill predators. A few species of millipedes, for example, ooze droplets that release a poisonous gas called hydrogen cyanide. Shutting one of these millipedes in a jar with other small living things will cause the animals to die from the fumes. The poison gas made by just one millipede can

The colorful, tiny poison dart frog can excrete poison from its skin when threatened.

kill more than six mice. Toads that seize such a millipede quickly spit it out. Some beetle larvae, centipedes, moths, and caterpillars also make hydrogen cyanide.

Poison dart frogs (also called poison arrow frogs), which live in Central and South America, excrete a poisonous, foul-tasting fluid from their skin when threatened. Some of these tiny frogs, which are small enough to perch on a quarter, produce poison strong enough to kill predators. In fact, they received their name from the fact that natives sometimes carefully extract the frogs' poison and coat the tips, or darts, of their arrows with it to catch and kill other animals. The most toxic is the golden frog. Just one drop of its poison can kill thousands of mice.

Of course, if a poisonous animal had a choice, it would rather not be attacked in the first place. It is better for it to stop an attack before it starts. A poisonous animal does this with warning colors, foul tastes, bad smells, irritating chemicals, and sometimes sounds.

WARNING COLORS

Bright colors help many animals find others of their species and communicate with them. They may also help hide animals in their habitats. Yet, bright colors can also be warning colors. Many animals that are poisonous, bad tasting, or both are clad in warning colors. The colors say to predators, "Don't even think of attacking me. You'll be sorry."

A predator that licks, mouths, or bites an animal with warning colors often drops or spits out its prey. The prey may taste bad, or irritate the predator's mouth. If the prey's poison is strong, it may also make the predator feel sick and throw up. After one or more experiences like this, the predator learns that it is a bad idea to attack this sort of prey. It is unlikely to go after another animal that looks like this disastrous meal.

Disgusting or sickening a predator in this way may be a better strategy for a prey animal than killing the predator. It is useful to have "educated" predators in the neighborhood—predators that will steer clear of the prey.

The most widely used warning colors are red, orange, yellow, black, or a combination of these. The iron-cross blister beetle, for example, has a black body, red head, and yellow wing covers marked with black bands. Like other blister beetles, it oozes irritating oil when seized by a predator. The oil causes blisters to form on the predator's skin.

Another noxious animal, the koppie foam grasshopper of South Africa, is black with red stripes. If it is attacked, a smelly, poisonous foam bubbles from its body. The foam not only makes the grasshopper taste bad, but it also is strong enough to kill a dog. Likewise, the lubber grasshopper of the southeastern United States is clad in warning colors of black and yellow. It also bubbles an irritating foam that is toxic enough to kill a bird. Opossums that swallow a lubber quickly throw it up.

Ladybugs with bright red shells and black dots are also wearing warning colors. The bright pattern signals that the ladybug may sicken or kill a small animal that eats it. A bird, lizard, or insect that ignores the warning and grabs the ladybug gets a second warning in the form of a smelly, bad-tasting yellow liquid that

A cinnabar caterpillar is foul tasting and poisonous, and its orange and black warning colors are meant to keep predators away.

oozes from the insect's joints. This oozing is called **reflex bleeding**. In addition to smelling and tasting awful, the fluid clogs up an insect predator's jaws. The ladybug's orange-and-black young also use reflex bleeding as a defense.

Moths, butterflies, and caterpillars that are poor-tasting or poisonous have warning colors as well. The white, black, and yellow caterpillar of the monarch butterfly, for example, is poisonous. The orange-and-black-striped caterpillars of the cinnabar moth are poisonous, too.

European magpie moths are boldly patterned at every stage of life. In their youth, their white, black, and red caterpillars ooze foul-tasting fluid that causes predators to spit them out. The caterpillars form cocoons that are glossy black and ringed with yellow stripes. The adult moths that hatch have white, black, and yellow markings.

AMPHIBIAN WARNING COLORS

Many salamanders, frogs, and other amphibians are also colored in red, black, yellow, and orange patterns. These bright colors also serve to warn predators to stay away.

The fire salamander of Europe, for example, is black with yellow spots or stripes. Sometimes red or orange tints appear on its skin, too. If a predator grabs it, poisonous fluids flow from the salamander's skin. The salamander can even squirt the poison.

Another amphibian, the fire-bellied toad, arches backward to reveal its bright red or yellow underside when it is bothered. A predator that grabs the toad anyway will quickly drop it after getting a taste of its poisonous skin—especially if the frightened toad has oozed so much poison that it seems to be covered in foam.

Poison dart frogs have a rainbow of warning colors. They may be red, orange, yellow, lime green, or cobalt blue, striped

POISONOUS BIRDS

In recent years, scientists have found that some birds might have warning colors—and that the birds are not only distasteful but also poisonous. The birds they studied live in rainforests in New Guinea.

One of these birds is the hooded pitohui, an orange bird with a black face and tail and black wings. In 1990, a researcher who licked his finger after being scratched by a pitohui reported that his tongue and lips tingled, burned, and then went numb for a few hours.

After more research, scientists found that the pitohui's feathers and skin contained poison. Smaller amounts of poison were also found in some of the birds' muscles and organs. Furthermore, it was the same kind of poison found in poison dart frogs.

People living in New Guinea's forests already knew to avoid the pitohui. They called it the "garbage bird" and told scientists that just being near it made them sneeze and made their noses, mouths, and eyes burn. People who ate the birds felt sick to their stomachs.

Scientists now want to find out how the birds became poisonous. They have found the same poison in a red-and-black beetle that pitohuis eat, so the birds might have become poisonous by eating poison themselves.

Since 1990, other species of poisonous pitohuis have been studied. Scientists have also found that another New Guinean bird, the blue-capped ifrita, contains the same poison. Again, the native people already knew this. Their word for this species means "bitter bird."

with black, depending on the species. Across the world in Africa, banded rubber frogs are clad in poisonous skins that are black with red stripes and spots. If attacked, they ooze a thick, sticky fluid that is poisonous to small predators and strong enough to irritate a human's skin.

Warning colors are even at work underwater, especially in the rainbow world of a coral reef. A slow-moving reef fish called the polka-dot boxfish, for example, stands out with its yellow skin dotted with black. This vivid skin spews sticky, poisonous mucus when the fish is attacked. If this is not enough to stop the attack, the boxfish's hard, boxy body protects it. Like most animals with warning colors, it is a sturdy creature that is hard to hurt or kill. It has to be, in order to survive while still teaching its predators a lesson.

SMELLS THAT REPEL

Colors that announce "I taste bad" or "I am poisonous" are often enough of a warning to potential predators. Just in case these animals fail to believe their eyes, warning smells may be sent to their noses as well. Animals that are well camouflaged may rely entirely on smelling bad.

Scientists have also found that these strong odors are usually accompanied by irritating chemicals. Just as a strong-smelling onion irritates a person's eyes, an animal's strong-smelling fluids can irritate a predator's eyes, nasal passages, lungs, or skin.

Strong odors are frequently used as a defense by many insects known as "true bugs." True bugs have beaklike mouthparts for piercing and sucking in food. Many of them also have stink glands. These stink glands are located on their backs when they are young and on their sides when they are adults.

The smelliest of all are the stink bugs. Stink bugs ooze a vile-smelling liquid if they are disturbed. The odor is described as smelling like a mixture of several pungent aromas—everything from licorice and overripe fruit to rotten eggs and skunk. It is strong enough to repel many birds, lizards, and other animals that eat insects.

Some stink bugs are brightly colored, such as the red and black two-spotted stink bug, but others are green or brown and blend in with their surroundings. Most walkingstick insects are also well camouflaged because they look like green or brown twigs. Not so the Peruvian walkingstick, which calls attention to itself with vivid red, black, and yellow markings. Its pattern warns "stay away," and so does the strong-smelling white fluid it oozes when it senses a threat. The fluid irritates any ant or spider that persists in trying to eat the walkingstick.

The caterpillars of different swallowtail butterfly species have warning colors, camouflage, or eyespots for startling predators.

If disturbed, stink bugs—like this spined stink bug—emit a strong almond smell that is offensive to many animals.

Some species also are poisonous. All have a forked, tongue-like body part that pops out from behind the head. It gives off a strong smell when the caterpillar is under threat. The smell of these caterpillars is often compared to dirty socks.

Other small animals also give off strong odors when threatened. A daddy longlegs puts out a smelly liquid from glands on its back when its body is grabbed. The liquid spreads across its body and repels attackers, such as ants.

Millipedes also give off strong odors if they are disturbed. Just the scent of some millipedes is enough to send ants scurrying

ONE WARNING FOR ALL

A gazelle that stamps its foot or stots (jumps high into the air) sends two important messages to a predator. First, the gazelle has seen the predator, so the predator has lost its chance to launch a surprise attack. Second, the gazelle is strong and healthy, so it would be a waste of time to chase it. This kind of warning is called pursuit deterrence.

Pursuit deterrence is different from *aposematism*, the use of warning colors or other signals to keep predators away. A gazelle that uses pursuit deterrence tells a predator that it is a strong, healthy individual at that particular moment. It does not mean that the predator should give up hunting gazelles altogether.

An aposematic animal, however, has a smell, taste, or color pattern that advertises how poor-tasting, poisonous, or dangerous it is—just like all the rest of its species. If a predator has tried to eat another individual of the same species in the past, it knows that this individual will present the same problems. Warning colors and other signals announce that every member of the species should be avoided at all times.

away. The strong odor comes from fluids that ooze from pores in the millipede's sides.

A millipede may let out fluid only from the pores close to the site of the attack. If this is not enough, it will discharge fluid from the rest of its pores, too. The fluid from some millipedes is not only smelly and irritating, but also sticky. Ants that attack such millipedes become slimed with the gluey fluids and must work hard to free themselves.

SPRAYING, SPITTING, AND SPEWING

Oozing, leaking, bubbling, and dripping toxic and irritating fluids can repel many predators. Some animals go one step further. Instead of letting predators get close enough to touch them, they keep them at bay by spraying, spitting, or otherwise spewing fluids at them.

Skunks are the most famous animals to use this tactic. A skunk has musk glands under its tail that can spray a terrible-smelling fluid at predators. Its white stripes are warning colors that are easily seen at night, when the skunk is active. An experienced predator knows to avoid it.

An inexperienced predator, however, gets a warning. Each species has its own way of saying "back off." A hooded skunk stamps its feet, then turns around to raise its tail and spray. A striped skunk also stamps and raises its tail, then curves sideways to aim its musk glands while keeping an eye on its foe. The spotted skunk stamps its front feet, then stands on them in a handstand and twists its back so that its musk glands are aimed at the predator.

Failure to heed these warnings earns the predator a blast in the face from the skunk's musk glands. A skunk can shoot its smelly spray 13 feet (4 m) and hit its target. The spray not only smells bad, but also irritates the predator's nose, mouth, and eyes. It can even temporarily blind the predator. After spraying, the skunk toddles off, leaving its victim pawing at its face.

Some snakes, such as the grass snake of Europe, have glands that release terrible-smelling fluid from their hind ends when they are caught. The green woodhoopoe, an African bird, pokes its tail out of its nest hole and sprays a smelly fluid from a gland at its base. The fluid, which smells worse than rotten eggs, repels predators such as snakes and rats. Other birds use droppings to repel enemies. A duck called the eider, for example, spews strong-smelling droppings on its eggs just before it flees from its nest if frightened by a predator.

Many kinds of beetles spray repulsive fluids from their hind ends, too. The darkling beetle of the southwestern United States reacts to a predator by practically standing on its head. Then it sprays fluid from the end of its abdomen. The spray repels ants, birds, lizards, and some rodents. A ground beetle of the southeastern United States sprays acid at ants that attack it. Carrion beetles, which feed on animal carcasses, also spray smelly, irritating fluid at ants, spiders, and other predators.

Many species of ants spray, too. Carpenter ants, for example, do not have stingers. Instead, they bite enemies with their jaws and then spray acid from their hind ends into the wounds. This acid is also used to kill the insects they eat.

The champion tail-tip sprayers among insects are bombardier beetles, found nearly worldwide. A bombardier beetle stores the different chemicals that make up its spray in different parts of its abdomen. If the beetle is attacked, it empties the chemicals stored in one part of its abdomen into the chamber that holds the rest of the brew. They combine to form an explosive, hot fluid that bursts out of the beetle's hind end with a loud pop.

A bombardier beetle can twist its abdomen to aim in nearly any direction. It can even shoot over its back. The hot, irritating spray repels ants, birds, and frogs.

Another insect, a walkingstick insect called the devil's rider, also uses a "cannon" to spray a terrible smelling fluid. Its defensive glands are located behind its head. Scientists who study this insect report that its spray irritates their lungs as well as their eyes. Like the bombardier, the devil's rider can spray in almost any direction. Unlike the bombardier, it does not wait for a bird to attack before defending itself. It sprays when the bird is still about 8 inches (20 cm) away.

Insects also use their mouths to shoot fluids at predators. Grasshoppers, for example, are known for their ability to spit. This "spit" is really the grasshopper's stomach contents. It is often mixed with poisonous substances from a part of the insect's throat called the crop. The lubber grasshopper of the southeastern United States, which is clad in warning colors of black and yellow, not only spits a dark-brown stream at predators, but also hisses at them and bubbles with irritating foam.

The larvae of insects called sawflies also spit up their stomach contents at predators. The larvae feed on eucalyptus trees in Australia, which contain an oil that stops most insects from eating its leaves. The oil is stored in a special pouch in a larva's body. If an ant, mouse, or bird attacks, the larva spits up the thick, strong-smelling goo. The larvae of some species that feed in groups will cluster together in a circle, with their heads facing out. Then the whole group spits up together.

Even some birds cough up stomach contents on predators. Many seabirds that nest on the ground, such as albatrosses, throw up their oily, fishy meals when a predator approaches. This defense behavior often is used by chicks. Birds or mammals that get hit will carry the terrible smell with them for days. They also may be chilly: Feathers and fur soaked with the fishy oil will do a poor job of keeping an animal warm in the cold places where many seabirds nest. Scientists who study these birds wear waterproof clothing when they are at work.

BORROWING POISON

Some poisonous animals make their own poison. Others use poison made by other living things. Scientists have discovered that these animals are able to eat poisonous meals and store the chemicals in their bodies for use in defense.

Monarch butterflies get their poison from milkweed plants, on which monarch caterpillars feed. Many kinds of milkweed make poison to defend themselves from plant-eating animals. The poison causes heart failure, and most animals avoid it. It does not, however, affect monarch caterpillars. As they grow, they stock up milkweed poison in their bodies. The poison remains after they turn into butterflies.

The foaming grasshoppers of Africa get their poison by eating milkweed, too. Other insects obtain poison from other plants. The garden tiger moth, for example, makes some of its poison but gets the rest from plants it eats as a caterpillar, such as poisonous foxgloves. Cinnabar moth caterpillars become poisonous by eating toxic ragwort plants. The caterpillar of the rattle-box moth also eats poisonous plants. The adult rattlebox moth, which has a warning coloration, is so distasteful that if it is caught in a web, the spider cuts it free.

Some insects get their poison by eating other poisonous insects. One kind of fire-colored beetle eats blister beetles and stores the defensive chemicals in its body. Some of the chemicals leak into a groove on its head. A female fire-colored beetle will accept a male as a mate only if he has a good supply of these chemicals. He will give her some of the chemical, which she will then pass on to her eggs. The chemical repels ants and other insects that might eat the eggs.

Cochineal insects, which feed on cactuses in American deserts, also make a defensive chemical that is stolen by other insects. This chemical, a red acid, repels ants and most other insects. But some insects are not bothered by it. One kind of moth caterpillar eats cochineal insects, and then when a predator bothers it, the moth caterpillar throws up the acid along with its stomach contents. Ants that get slimed with this substance give up their attack. The larva of a species of ladybug also eats cochineal insects. Its body uses the bug's acid as part of the beetle's reflex-bleeding defense. The larvae of a fly species that eat cochineal insects excrete the acid to repel predators.

Other animals can eat poisonous bugs without being harmed, and then use the poison themselves. Poison dart frogs do not actually make their own poison; they get it from the insects they eat. Their most likely source is a beetle. Poisonous pitohui birds may eat relatives of this beetle.

A kind of Asian grass snake called the tiger keelback uses poison taken from its prey for defense, too. The snake eats toads that are poisonous. Its body stores the poison in glands on its neck. When a predator threatens it, the snake does not flee. Instead, it tucks in its head to present the poison-filled glands. If the predator bites, it will get a mouthful of poison.

PREDATORS OF POISONOUS PREY

Warning colors, bad tastes, foul smells, and poison—these defenses protect their owners from many predators, but not all. Some predators are able to eat them without suffering any harm.

Sometimes, this ability comes from a natural resistance to the poison. One kind of tropical snake, for example, can eat poison dart frogs and not be harmed. It is affected only by large amounts of toxin from the most poisonous species of frogs.

Likewise, the European hedgehog eats toads and is not affected by the poison in their skin glands. It is even known to chew on the poisonous skin and then spread the poisonous fluid onto its own spiny body. The mongoose, a mammal that lives in Africa and Asia, eats poisonous snakes and toads, too.

Some birds are resistant to defensive chemicals, too. The black-headed grosbeak eats monarch butterflies. Another bird, the northern shrike, stabs monarchs onto thorns and branches and lets them rot for a few days. The poison in the prey breaks down, and then the bird eats it.

Some predators can eat prey by avoiding their unpleasant fluids. A great horned owl, for example, can snatch up a skunk so quickly that it doesn't have time to spray—and even if it does, the stink doesn't bother the owl, which has little to no sense of smell. A species of true bug that eats meat instead of plants has an extra-long beak, which it uses to pierce insect larvae. Thanks to the length of this beak, the bug's head and body never come close to the nasty fluid that oozes from its prey. A big toad can eat a millipede that oozes poisonous droplets, if it grabs the millipede quickly and swallows it instantly.

The grasshopper mouse of Southwestern deserts avoids the smelly spray of the darkling beetle with a neat trick: It shoves the beetle's hind end into the sand. Then the mouse eats the beetle headfirst. Spiders use a similar tactic when they catch bombardier beetles in their webs. A spider that has snared one of these explosive beetles moves slowly and carefully as it ties up the beetle with silk. Once the beetle is tightly wrapped, the spider will eat it.

Predators also can avoid defense chemicals by removing them from their prey. Some birds, such as blue jays, remove the head

A coati will use its front paws to roll up poisonous millipedes, an action that gets rid of the defensive chemicals millipedes may release.

and digestive tract of lubber grasshoppers before eating them. Without these parts, the insect is safe to eat.

Animals called coatis, which live in parts of the southwestern United States and in Central and South America, use their front paws to roll poisonous millipedes across the ground. The millipedes ooze defensive chemicals, but they are wiped away by the rolling. Then the coatis crunch up the millipedes. Another mammal, the little angwantibo of western Africa, rubs off the irritating hairs of the caterpillars that make up its diet.

5

Venomous Stings and Bites

VENOM IS A POISON made by an animal's body and injected into another animal. A venomous animal has a sting, spines, or specialized teeth attached to venom-making glands. A poisonous animal, on the other hand, must usually be touched or eaten by another animal for the poison to work. A poisonous animal often has a bad taste, foul smell, or bright color pattern warning that it is dangerous to eat.

Some venomous animals use venom to catch their own prey. They subdue or kill their prey by biting or stinging it. Snakes, wasps, and spiders are examples of animals that catch prey in this way. On the other hand, honeybees do not. They use their venom only for defense.

Like poisonous animals, some venomous animals exhibit warning colors. Many venomous animals, however, are camouflaged. This helps them sneak up on prey.

Many animals' venom is strong enough only to harm or kill its smaller prey. But some venom can harm or even kill much larger animals, too. Some of the world's stinging animals have this powerful venom.

VENOMOUS STINGS

Packed inside an insect no bigger than a jellybean is a venom strong enough to cause intense pain in humans—and occasionally death, in people who are allergic to it. This venom belongs to the honeybee.

A female honeybee has an abdomen tipped with a sting. The bee's vivid pattern of black and yellow stripes warns birds and other predators that she is armed and dangerous.

Nearly all bees in a hive are females, which take care of a queen bee that lays all the hive's eggs. If their hive is threatened, these worker bees use their stings to repel the intruder.

A honeybee's stinger is attached to a pouch of venom in its abdomen. The bee stings by jabbing its stinger into a predator's skin. Sawlike parts on the stinger dig their way into the flesh. When the bee flies away, part of its abdomen is yanked off in the process. The bee soon dies, but the venom-filled pouch remains behind, pumping venom through the firmly embedded stinger and into its victim.

The bee also gives off scent signals when it stings. These scent signals are called **pheromones**. Other worker bees that sense the pheromone become alarmed. They rush to the defense of their hive and queen.

Honeybees do not use their venom to kill prey because they feed on pollen and nectar made by flowers. Their venom is used only for defense. Wasps and many ants, however, use their venom for hunting as well as defending themselves.

Like bees, many wasps make loud buzzing sounds as they fly, and many of them wear warning colors. Both the sounds and the colors signal "danger" to birds, mammals, and many other predators. Wasps sting to protect themselves. Species of wasps that nest in groups also sting to defend their nests.

Unlike a bee's sting, a wasp's sting does not get stuck in a predator's flesh. A wasp can sting repeatedly, with each sting causing great pain. The red velvet ant, a kind of wasp with black and orange-red markings, is also known as a "cow killer." That's because people say the pain from its sting is strong enough to kill a cow.

Just as with bees, only female wasps have stings. This is because the sting evolved from a body part called an ovipositor, which is used for laying eggs. A male wasp does not lay eggs, so it lacks an ovipositor.

Predatory wasps use their venom to kill prey ranging from tiny insects to spiders. This prey is chewed up and fed to their larvae. Yellowjackets are predatory wasps. They have bold stripes of black and yellow, white, or red, depending on the species. Their prey includes insects such as grasshoppers and caterpillars that harm crops. A few species of yellowjacket are scavengers—animals that eat prey that has been killed by other animals. These are the yellowjackets that are nuisances at picnics.

Many kinds of ants also have stings for killing other insects. Some species, such as army ants found in tropical forests of Central and South America, feed only on other insects. Other species use their venom mainly for defense. This venom can be extremely powerful. A group of army ants can kill a snake, though they do not eat it.

Stinging ants first bite a predator so that they can hang on to it with their jaws. Then they jab their stings into the predator's skin. Ants that do not have stings also grip skin with their jaws. Then they spray the wound with a blast of venom from their abdomens.

Another animal with a venomous sting is the scorpion. Scorpions are in a group of animals called arachnids. This group also includes spiders and ticks. There are about 1,500 species of scorpions, and they are found nearly worldwide. These nocturnal animals use venom for both hunting and defense.

HOW VENOM WORKS

An animal's venom is made up of many substances. The mixture of substances is different for each venomous species, though different mixtures include some of the same poisonous substances.

Different venoms affect the body in different ways. Some venoms affect the brain and the nerves. This kind of venom is called a neurotoxin. A neurotoxin may make muscles cramp or twitch. It may also paralyze muscles, which can make an animal stop breathing and lead to heart failure. Other venoms harm the blood. They are called hemotoxins. A hemotoxin may cause bleeding inside the body, or it can make the blood **clot** too quickly or too slowly. Venoms can also cause swelling, severe rashes, and other reactions.

The body of a venomous animal uses energy to make venom. This is why venomous animals prefer to hide or flee from danger. An animal that makes venom for killing prey would rather save its venom for hunting and not waste it on an animal it cannot eat. Even an animal that makes venom only for self-defense is usually slow to use it. It is more likely to hide, flee, or warn a predator to stay away.

Scientists have developed substances that can stop venoms from damaging the body. These substances are called antivenins. Antivenins exist for many, but not all venoms. They have saved many lives. Venoms are actually used in making the antivenins. Scientists are also researching venoms to find substances that can be used to make medicines. The venom of the cone snail, for example, has yielded a drug that is used as a painkiller.

Scorpions eat insects, snails, pillbugs, and spiders. Some species eat lizards and mice, too. A scorpion can often overpower its prey by grabbing it in its claws. If the prey struggles, the scorpion curls its tail over its back and stings it.

Most scorpions' stings are only mildly painful to humans, but about 25 species have venom strong enough to kill a person. Besides using their venom to kill prey, scorpions also will sting to defend themselves against predators, such as birds, rats, lizards, centipedes, and other scorpions. Yet, a scorpion's primary defense is camouflage. Tan, brown, and black coloring helps scorpions hide in their habitats.

STINGING TENTACLES

A group of ocean animals called cnidarians also use stings for predation and self-defense. This group includes corals, jellyfish, and anemones. Most are harmless to humans, or cause little more than a rash. Some cnidarians, however, contain venom strong enough to sicken or kill a human. The box jelly, also called a sea wasp, is among the most deadly. It lives off the coast of Australia. Its venom causes extreme pain, and a bad sting can kill a human in less than five minutes.

Cnidarians' stingers are called **nematocysts**. They are located on the animals' tentacles. Hundreds or even thousands of nematocysts can be found on one tentacle, depending on the species. A box jelly's tentacle, which can be 9 feet (3 meters) long, contains millions of nematocysts.

There are three kinds of nematocysts. One kind makes a gluey substance that sticks to prey. A second kind shoots out threads that loop around prey like coils of rope. The third kind is venomous and works like a miniature harpoon. An animal may have one or more kinds, depending on its species.

When an animal—either predator or prey—comes in contact with a tentacle with venomous nematocysts, the nematocysts launch their harpoons. Out shoots a tiny barb attached to a twisted thread. The barb jabs the animal's body. The thread untwists, pushing the barb into the skin. Venom flows through the thread and into the animal.

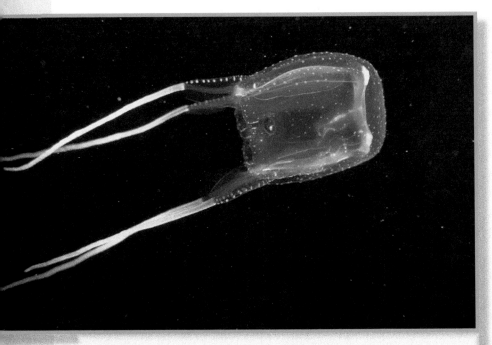

A sting from a sea wasp can kill a person in less than five minutes.

The venom paralyzes or kills prey so that the cnidarian can drag it to its mouth and eat it. Cnidarians eat a variety of prey, depending on their size. Anemones look like plants rooted in sand and mud or on rocks and coral reefs. However, they are animals, and they feed on small fish, crabs, and shrimp. Coral polyps, which make up coral reefs, feed on tiny animals called zooplankton that drift in the water. Many jellyfish feed on fish and shrimp.

VENOMOUS SPINES

Prickly hairs, spikes, quills, and spines on an animal's body help defend it. They can be irritating or painful, or difficult to swallow. Among the ranks of these bristly beasts are animals whose spines also are venomous.

Caterpillars of different species, for example, often have barbed hairs as part of their defense systems. The hairs irritate predators. Some species' hairs also are attached to venom glands. These hairs not only pierce predators, but also inject venom. Often a predator is jabbed merely by touching the caterpillar. Some kinds of caterpillars arch their bodies to stab their spines into a predator as it attacks.

The saddleback caterpillar is a bristly brown caterpillar with a green "saddle blanket" on its back. When its hairs are touched, they stick in the predator's skin and their tips break off, allowing venom to flow out from the caterpillar's body

BORROWING VENOM

Some sea creatures, such as coral-eating parrotfish and jellyfish-eating sea turtles, prey on cnidarians. Most animals, of course, avoid them. Yet, a few animals have found ways to use the cnidarians' venom for their own self-defense.

Anemonefish live safely among the tentacles of anemones. The fishes' scales are covered with a protective slime that keeps the anemones from hurting them. Anemonefish guard the anemones by chasing away other animals. Other fish find safety by living among the tentacles of jellyfish.

Some kinds of sea slugs are also protected by slime—but instead of living among an anemone's tentacles, they eat them. Instead of digesting the nematocysts, however, the sea slug's body stores them in frills or bumps along its back. There, they work to protect the sea slug from predators.

through the hollow hairs. Saddlebacks are found in the eastern United States. A saddleback's sting causes pain and swelling at the site of the sting, and can make a person feel nauseated.

Flannel moth caterpillars also have venomous hairs. The fuzzy caterpillars look soft enough to pet, but their powerful venom causes severe pain and swelling. Some flannel moth caterpillars in South America have such strong venom that they can temporarily paralyze a human. In Brazil, they are known as "fire beasts" because of their painful sting. Another South American caterpillar, the larva of the giant silkworm moth, inflicts stings that can be deadly to humans.

Venomous spines also are found on a number of sea creatures, such as stingrays. Stingrays are flat-bodied cousins of

A sharp, venomous spine on a stingray's tail helps it defend itself from predators, such as sharks.

sharks. They hunt for clams, worms, and other prey on the seabed in shallow water, and often half-bury themselves in sand and mud when resting. Their tails are armed with sharp spines that are notched along their edges like saw blades.

Stingrays use their spines to defend themselves from predators, such as sharks. A frightened stingray lashes its spiny tail over its back to sting its foe. It also stings people who step on it.

Fireworms, some sea urchins, and the crown-of-thorns starfish also rely on sharp, venomous spines for protection. The fireworm is covered with hollow bristles that break off easily in a predator's skin and allow venom to seep into it. The burning pain that results gives the fireworm its name. A fireworm warns that it is dangerous by flaring its bristles.

A sea urchin is a prickly pincushion at all times. An urchin's spines pierce and break off in a predator's skin. Venomous long-spined sea urchins give predators a dose of venom as well as an injury, because venom flows from the broken spines. Some species' spines are covered with venomous skin, which leaks venom when the spine stabs an animal. The crown-of-thorns starfish, a relative of urchins, also delivers its venom in this way.

An urchin, which can sense light and dark, can pinpoint its attacker and then aim its spines in that direction. The most venomous urchin, called the flower urchin, has nonvenomous spines. However, it has miniature sets of venomous jaws hidden among its spines.

Other species have venomous spines in their fins. Like stingrays, these fish use their spines only for defense. The weeverfish, found along British beaches, hunts by lying hidden in the sand in shallow water. It has venomous spines in its back fin and over its gills. It doesn't use these on the shrimp and small fish that it snaps up as they swim by, but a fish that tries to eat the weeverfish will be confronted by these weapons.

A large stars-and-stripes toadfish swims over a coral reef. Toadfish use their venomous spines against predators, and their camouflaged body color and spines help them hunt prey.

Venomous toadfish nestle in sand in the warm, shallow waters of Central and South America. Like weevers, they sport venomous spines on their backs and gill covers. Their drab, brown-and-gray coloring helps camouflage them as they lie in wait to catch fish and other small prey with their wide, toothy mouths. The hollow spines are used only for injecting venom into predators.

Another well-camouflaged fish of shallow ocean water is the warty, slow-moving stonefish. It releases venom when the spines in its back fin are pressed. The venom shoots along grooves in the spines and into the injury caused by the pointy tips. Stone-fish live in parts of the Indian and western Pacific oceans. Their venom is the deadliest of any fish. People get stung when they accidentally step on a stonefish. Sharks and rays get stung when they close their jaws on one.

Not all venomous fish are sluggish, bottom-dwelling species. The gaudy lionfish, with its bright colors and large fins, is a vivid sight as it swims among other coral reef fish. Its beautiful fins, however, contain venomous spines. A lionfish uses them to defend itself and will turn to face a predator, spreading out its spiny fins in warning.

Worldwide, there are about 1,200 kinds of venomous fish—more than twice the number of venomous snake species.

A lionfish spreads out its venomous spiny fins in warning.

VENOMOUS BITES

Venomous snakes inject their venom by biting, as do spiders, centipedes, octopuses, and a few lizards and mammals. All of these animals use their venom to paralyze or kill their prey, as well as to defend against predators.

There are about 500 species of venomous snakes worldwide. Only a few are deadly to humans. Among them are cobras, which are found in parts of Africa and Asia.

Cobras prey on rodents, birds, frogs, lizards, snakes, and other small animals. A cobra kills prey with venom produced in glands at the back of its jaws, near its eyes. The venom flows down grooves in the fangs at the front of its mouth.

The biggest cobra, the king cobra, is also the world's largest venomous snake. The largest king cobra ever measured was 18 feet (5.6 m) long. However, the king cobra, like other venomous snakes, is not eager to use its venom in self-defense. It is more likely to flee or hide, even though its venom is strong enough to kill an elephant with just one bite. If a predator approaches the cobra or its nest, the cobra raises the front of its body off the ground and hisses. It also spreads the ribs of its neck, creating a hood out around its head. If these warnings are ignored, the snake strikes.

Some cobras spray venom at predators instead of biting them. These "spitting cobras" have openings midway down their front fangs. The snake squeezes venom through these openings. The spray can hit a target up to 10 feet (3 m) away. It usually ends up in the predator's eyes, causing terrible pain and blindness. Sometimes, the blindness is permanent.

Rattlesnakes, like cobras, deliver their venom with fangs. However, a rattlesnake's fangs are not fixed in place like a cobra's. Instead, they are hinged. They fold back in the rattlesnake's mouth when it is closed. When the snake opens its mouth to strike, the fangs spring out, ready for action.

This juvenile king cobra is giving off a warning sign by hissing.

A rattlesnake's colors and patterns help camouflage it. If it is spotted by a predator, the rattlesnake will try to slither away from danger. Yet, if a predator bothers it, the rattlesnake coils up and rattles its hollow, scaly tail sections.

Another venomous North American snake, the cottonmouth or water moccasin, sends a warning by stretching open its white-lined mouth. The world's deadliest snake, the black mamba of Africa, also warns away enemies by opening its black-lined mouth. A recently discovered species of venomous snake in Asia is able to change colors. This behavior has earned it the name "chameleon snake." Scientists think the color changes may be a warning to predators.

Some kinds of snakes, such as coral snakes, are clad in warning colors that advertise their venomous nature. Coral snakes are ringed with bands of black, red, and either white or yellow. These relatives of cobras live in North, Central, and South America, where they prey mainly on lizards and other snakes.

Unlike snakes, the world's two species of venomous lizards use their venom mainly for self-defense, not hunting. The Mexican beaded lizard and its smaller cousin, the Gila (pronounced "heela") monster, are both slow-moving animals that feed mainly on eggs, baby rodents, and baby birds found in nests on the ground. If disturbed, these lizards bite with their strong jaws. Venom flows through the teeth from glands in their lower jaws. The lizards chew their victims so the venom sinks inside them. Both species have bright warning colors: They are black, with yellow or pink uneven bands.

Vivid warning colors also adorn venomous centipedes, such as the giant Sonoran centipede. This many-legged animal, which lives in some of the same desert lands as the Gila monster, can grow to be 8 inches (20 cm) long and is boldly patterned in orange and black. It bites insects, worms, frogs, and other prey with a pair of sharp, claw-like fangs near its head. Muscles squeeze venom out of a gland in each fang. Like snakes, centipedes use venom for defense as well as hunting.

Spiders' venom also does double duty. Many spiders catch their prey in webs, then deliver a killing bite with their fangs. Hunting spiders lie in wait for their prey, or prowl about in search of prey and then pounce on it like a tiger. They hang on to their prey with their legs while they bite it, killing it with venom.

Spiders also bite predators that attack them. Most spiders' fangs are not strong enough to pierce predators' skin, though, and the venom is not strong enough to harm. A few spiders do have powerful venom. The black widow spider's venom is more potent than many snakes' venom. The brown recluse spider has venom strong enough to make a person feel ill for several days. Like all spiders, however, these species would rather hide from danger than bite someone.

Octopuses also would rather hide, but they will bite if they are stepped on or attacked. An octopus uses its venom and its strong, sharp beak to kill crabs, fish, and other prey. Most octopus venom is not strong enough to do great harm to humans, but the venom of blue-ringed octopuses can kill.

Different species of blue-ringed octopuses live in parts of the Indian Ocean and the western Pacific Ocean. Normally, they wear camouflaging colors of brown, gray, and pale yellow. But if they are disturbed, bright blue rings suddenly appear. These rings are warning colors—and the warning is not a bluff.

A greater blue-ringed octopus makes one kind of venom for hunting and another kind for self-defense. This little octopus, which is no bigger than a golf ball, contains enough venom to kill about 25 people in just a few minutes. Most people harmed by a blue-ringed octopus have either picked it up or stepped on it.

The ocean contains another group of animals that are among the world's most venomous animals: the cone snails. There are about 600 species of cone snail. Most are found in tropical waters and on coral reefs. Only a small number contain venom that is deadly to humans.

Cone snails use their venom to kill prey, such as worms, snails, and fish. The venom is delivered by a bite that works much like a sting or harpoon. The snail shoots out a tube attached to a sharp, hollow tooth. Venom flows from a gland in the snail through this tube and into the prey. The snail uses its venom in self-defense when it is attacked by a hungry fish.

PREDATORS OF VENOMOUS ANIMALS

Many animal species have changed over time so that they can eat poisonous animals and plants without harm. In the same way, some animals have evolved to hunt and eat venomous animals.

Bumblebees are venomous and can sting repeatedly, like wasps. Yet skunks, foxes, badgers, and other mammals will raid

VENOMOUS MAMMALS

The use of venom is common among insects, snakes, and other animal families. No birds are known to be venomous, and there are only a few species of venomous mammals.

Venomous bites are found in a few species of small mammals called shrews. They use their venomous saliva to paralyze or kill prey, such as mice, fish, frogs, and newts. They also will bite in self-defense, leaving their attacker with pain and swelling. Another mammal with venomous saliva for killing prey is the solenodon. This animal looks like a shrew. It lives only on the islands of Cuba and Hispaniola in the West Indies.

The platypus of Australia is also venomous. This duck-billed, beaver-tailed mammal has no teeth, but the male platypus has venomous spurs on its hind legs. They are used for defense and for fighting with other males. The venom is said to be strong enough to kill a dog.

The slow loris, a chubby, big-eyed animal of southeast Asia, also uses venom to protect itself. A loris's venom gland is in its arm. To use the venom, the loris licks its arm. Then, when it bites, the mixture of saliva and venom seeps out from between its teeth into the wound. The smell of the venomous saliva repels predators, such as bears. This may be why a female loris spreads saliva on her young when she needs to leave them untended for a while.

bumblebee nests, risking stings as they dig up and eat bee lar-vae and stored food. Bears raid the nests of honeybees as well as bumblebees. Bees visiting flowers may be snared by crab spiders lying in wait for them among the blossoms. Some kinds of wasps specialize in hunting bees to feed to their young.

A variety of birds also feed on bees, taking care to remove the sting or venom first. Bee-eaters, found in Europe, Africa, Asia, and Australia, catch bees in midair with their long beaks. A bee-eater that catches a bee perches in a tree, where it rubs and bashes its prey against a branch until the venom and sting are squeezed out. Then the bee-eater safely eats its meal.

South American birds called motmots use this method, too. In North America, birds called northern shrikes can eat bees and wasps. A shrike rubs the insect on a branch or jams it onto a thorn and pulls out the sting with its beak.

Long-billed birds of Africa and Asia called hornbills eat venomous snakes, centipedes, and scorpions. A hornbill will grasp the prey with the tip of its beak and then squeeze the prey from one end to the other. By the time the birds are through, all the venom glands have been squashed and the stingers destroyed.

Baboons and other African monkeys eat scorpions. They remove the scorpion's tail, then eat the rest of the body. African mammals called meerkats teach their pups how to bite off scorpions' stingers.

Even venomous snakes get eaten. The long-legged secretary bird of Africa will kick a snake and stomp on it to kill it. Mongooses, which are in the same family as meerkats, kill and eat deadly cobras. With strong jaws, a mongoose quickly grabs a snake behind its head. Mongooses also dine on other venomous animals, such as spiders, scorpions, and centipedes.

Mongooses are partly resistant to the venom of snakes. Opossums, European hedgehogs, and some rodents also are resistant to the venom of certain snakes. King snakes, which are not venomous, are immune to other snakes' venom. They are known to eat rattlesnakes, copperheads, and other venomous snakes. Frogs tolerate the stings of the ants that they eat, as do the horned lizards of North American deserts.

6

Mimicry

A YELLOW AND BLACK insect approaches a flower. Its wings make a loud buzzing sound as it hovers above the petals. A toad, hiding under a nearby leaf, sees the insect, but makes no move to nab it. Once, it gobbled up a bumblebee and was stung on its tongue. This painful experience taught the toad a lifelong lesson.

What the toad does not know is that this insect is not really a bumblebee. It is a harmless American hover fly—an insect that would make a fine meal for a toad. To the toad, the insect's color, sound, and behavior all warn "bumblebee." If the toad could talk, it would probably mutter, "Better safe than sorry."

The hover fly is a **mimic**—an animal that looks like another kind of animal and benefits from this resemblance. The hover fly gains protection from predators by looking like a bee. Mimicry also includes sounding, smelling, acting, or otherwise resembling another animal. Scientists call the animal that is being mimicked the **model**.

Mimicry is different from the imitating used by animals to hide. An insect that looks like a leaf, for example, is imitating something that does not interest a predator. It is hidden, or camouflaged, by being a leaf look-alike. An insect that looks and acts like a bee, however, is not hiding. It is imitating a living thing

The harmless hover fly benefits from looking just like a sting-ready bumblebee.

that a predator could eat. At the same time, it warns the predator not to attack.

The study of mimicry dates back to the mid-1800s. Scientists found two kinds of mimicry among animals. First, some harmless animals mimic harmful ones. This kind of mimicry became known as **Batesian mimicry**. Second, some harmful animals mimic other harmful species. This kind of mimicry became known as **Müllerian mimicry**.

Since then, scientists have learned much more about mimicry. They have found animals that mimic their prey in order to hunt them, venomous animals that mimic less harmful animals, and other animals that mimic animals in order to live inside their nests. Scientists have learned that mimics and models may form

THE DISCOVERERS OF MIMICRY

The two main types of mimicry, Batesian and Müllerian, are named after the scientists who first suggested them: Henry Bates and Fritz Müller.

Henry Bates was an English naturalist who lived from 1825 to 1892. In 1848, he traveled to South America to study insects. Bates spent 11 years in the Amazon rainforest. He collected thousands of insects, about half of which had never been seen by scientists before.

During his stay, Bates noticed that some species of nonpoisonous butterflies looked very much like the brightly colored, poisonous butterflies in the same area. He realized that the edible butterflies were mimicking the poisonous ones. Bates wrote about his discoveries in 1862.

His work inspired other researchers. One of them was Fritz Müller, a German scientist. Müller followed up on a puzzle that Bates had noticed in Brazil. Bates had seen poisonous butterflies that belonged to different species, but resembled one another. Müller published a paper in 1878 explaining that by looking alike, both species shared the burden of teaching predators to leave them alone. The evolution of similar appearances benefits both species because each one loses fewer individuals than it would if it had to deal with predators on its own. That evolution would happen because butterflies with lookalike colors and patterns would have a better chance of survival and would produce more young than butterflies that didn't.

large, complex patterns known as mimicry rings. They have even found mimicry in plants. Yet, many of the animal world's mimics still fit into the two categories discovered more than 100 years ago.

INSECTS AND BATESIAN MIMICRY

The concept of Batesian mimicry was first revealed by studies of butterflies. It was later found in many other insects.

Bees and wasps are among the most commonly mimicked insects. Mimics of these stinging insects are found in several different, unrelated families of insects.

The yellow-and-black American hover fly is one of many flies that mimic bees. For starters, there are about 6,000 other species in the hover fly's insect family. Most of these species look like bees or wasps. Some species even hold up their front legs when they land and wave them around. This makes their legs look like antennae.

Another group of flies that also contains bee mimics is the aptly named bee-fly family. Bee flies are plump, fuzzy flies that resemble bees and also hover above flowers. A third fly family, the robber flies, mimics bees and wasps but preys on other insects, including bees.

Some kinds of beetles mimic bees and wasps. A North American beetle called the flat-headed bald cypress sapwood borer has wasp-like black and yellow stripes. These stripes are on the hard front pair of wings that all beetles have.

Most beetles hold up these wings (called elytra) and use a second pair of wings to fly. But the borer does not. It keeps its elytra clamped down while flying, so it still looks like a wasp. Birds seem to like to eat this beetle, but its wasp-like markings help repel them. Other species related to the borer also mimic wasps.

Bee and wasp mimics also exist among some kinds of moths that are active during the day. The hornet moth, for example, looks like a kind of wasp called a hornet. The yellow-banded sphinx and the bumblebee moth both mimic bees.

Ants are commonly mimicked, too. They are included with wasps and bees in a large group called the order Hymenoptera. Many ants bite or sting and contain an irritating, distasteful fluid called formic acid. These defenses cause many insects and other predators to avoid ants—and other animals to mimic them.

Some species of jumping spiders have two-part bodies that look more like the three-part bodies of ants. They also hold up their front legs so that they look like waving antennae. This leaves

They may look like ants, but jumping spiders are actually mimicking them. Here, two ants flank a jumping spider.

them with six legs for running and darting in an antlike manner. Species of beetles, flies, plant-sucking bugs, and the young of various insects also mimic ants.

Lycid beetles are also often mimicked. There are about 3,000 species of this beetle worldwide. Most smell bad, taste bad, and wear warning colors of orange and black. Birds avoid eating them. Batesian mimics of lycid beetles include some species of flies, the South American cockroach, and even other beetles.

Another beetle model is the tiger beetle, which bites with strong jaws. Among its mimics are the harmless young of the Malaysian katydid, a relative of the grasshopper and cricket. Some species of grasshoppers imitate tiger beetles, too.

Other grasshoppers mimic bombardier beetles, which can spray attackers with a jet of boiling hot fluid. Harmless cockroaches mimic ladybugs. One species of cockroach has wings that curl up so that it looks short and round, like a ladybug.

Butterflies, the insects that originally inspired the study of mimicry, still fascinate scientists with their complex mimic-and-model relationships. The pipevine swallowtail is a beautiful blue-and-black butterfly with yellow, orange, and white spots sprinkled on the edges and undersides of its wings. It is found in the eastern United States and parts of Mexico. Pipevine swallowtail caterpillars feed on poisonous pipevine plants, storing the poison. The adult butterflies taste bad and are poisonous. A bird that eats a pipevine swallowtail gets sick. The bird remembers the butterfly's warning colors and avoids it in future. Such birds also avoid the pipevine swallowtail's otherwise-tasty mimics: female spicebush swallowtails, red-spotted purples, and female Diana fritillaries.

Another model for Batesian mimics is the common crow butterfly, a black, brown, and white bad-tasting butterfly found in Asia. The confused clearwing, a butterfly of South America, also tastes bad. It is mimicked by two other species of butterfly, as well as a moth.

One of the most dazzling mimics among butterflies is the African swallowtail. Females of this species have different colors; they mimic different bad-tasting butterflies, depending on where they live. In one area, females are orange, black, and white. In

THE MIMIC OCTOPUS

The mimic octopus is named for its stunning ability to mimic not one, but at least three dangerous animals that share its tropical ocean home. It can strike poses and change colors to make itself look like a venomous lionfish, a venomous sea snake, and a poisonous fish called the banded sole.

Like other octopuses, the mimic octopus can easily change the shape and color of its rubbery body. Many octopuses use these abilities to camouflage themselves, squeeze into hiding places, and communicate with one another. The mimic octopus, however, is the first species known to imitate dangerous sea creatures to defend itself.

To imitate the sole, the octopus pulls its eight arms together into a wedge-shaped bundle and jets forward. This makes it look like a flat-bodied sole rippling through the water. To mimic a lionfish, the octopus spreads out its arms and lets them dangle so that they look like the lionfish's venomous, flared fins. It mimics a sea snake by changing its brown and white stripes to black and yellow, then tucking most of its body and all but two of its arms into a burrow. The two exposed arms wriggle and squirm like writhing sea snakes.

The mimic's performances have been caught on film. Researchers suspect that the octopus may mimic stingrays, jellyfish, and other sea animals.

another, they are black, yellow, and white. In another area, they are white and black. There are more than a dozen color combinations in this species.

OTHER BATESIAN MIMICS

Batesian mimicry is common among insects. It is also common in many other **invertebrates**.

Some of the most remarkable mimics in this group are nudibranchs. A nudibranch is a kind of sea slug. Nudibranchs eat algae, anemones, coral polyps, and sponges. Some species also eat other nudibranchs. Their colorful meals provide much of their own color. This helps some species blend in with their surroundings.

Many nudibranchs store the venomous stings or bad-tasting poisons of their prey and use them in their own defense. Predators learn that the colors of these nudibranchs are warning colors. They learn to leave them alone. Other nudibranchs mimic the colors of the dangerous nudibranchs, and so do ocean-dwelling flatworms.

Batesian mimicry also appears in **vertebrates**. It is particularly widespread in fish. The common sole, for example, is a European fish with a fin on its back that is edged in black. It mimics the weeverfish, which has venomous black spines in its back fin. Both fish are well camouflaged by color and shape as they hide in mud and sand underwater but raise their black-edged fins as a warning when disturbed. Poisonous flatworms and venomous sea urchins and sea snakes are also mimicked by fish.

One of the most remarkable fish mimics is a harmless species called the comet, which lives on coral reefs of the Indian Ocean and western Pacific Ocean. The comet is black with white spots. When threatened by a predator, it dives into a crack in the reef, leaving its hind end sticking out. Then the fish raises the fins on its tail, back, and underside. This reveals a large black spot surrounded by a white ring. Now the comet's hind end looks almost exactly like the head of a whitemouth moray eel, a ferocious predator that lurks in crevices on the reef.

Some reptiles also use mimicry. In southern Africa, a bushveld lizard is camouflaged when fully grown, but it has black with white spots and a dull red tail when it is young. This makes the young lizard's small body look like that of an oogpister beetle, which sprays a smelly, burning fluid at predators. The little lizard even walks like a beetle, with its tail held down so that it blends in with the sand.

Scientists have found lizards in South America that mimic invertebrates, too. One species of lizard curls its tail over its back to show its orange underside when it is bothered. This makes it look like a venomous scorpion. Another kind of South American lizard has young that look like a poisonous millipede.

Some caterpillars mimic snakes, as do other snakes. The false cobra of Asia, for example, is mildly venomous—its bite is not deadly like a cobra's. But when it is bothered, the false cobra rises up, spreads its neck like a hood, and hisses loudly, just as the real cobra does.

In North America, non-venomous bull snakes mimic rattlesnakes. A bull snake does not have a rattle, but if threatened, it will shake its tail rapidly. This rustles the leaves and grass around it, and can startle a predator into thinking that it is dealing with a rattlesnake.

The most famous example of snake mimicry centers on coral snakes. There are about 65 species of coral snakes found in parts of North, Central, and South America. They are highly venomous and clad in warning colors of black and red with yellow or white bands. Snakes that share these colors are known as false coral snakes. Some false coral snakes are mildly venomous. Others, such as the scarlet king snake, are non-venomous.

For many years, scientists assumed that the coral snake was the model and the other snakes were mimics. However, it may be that the mildly venomous false coral snakes are the models. A bite from such a snake would hurt a predator, but not kill it. The predator would learn to avoid such snakes in the future. These would create a population of "educated" predators that have learned to avoid red, yellow, and black snakes.

A bite from a deadly coral snake, however, would kill the predator. This would mean that the coral snake could never "educate" predators to leave it alone. Thus, the deadly snake may mimic the less deadly one—it benefits from having the less deadly snake educate the predators. The non-venomous mimics benefit, too.

MIMICRY IN MAMMALS

Mimicry is not widely found in birds or mammals. Yet, there are a few examples.

The African porcupine may be a model for a large African rodent called the maned rat. The porcupine has sharp, black-and-white quills that are easily seen as it moves about at night. Its mimic, the maned rat, is also most active at night. It lacks quills, but has a mane of black fur on its back that it can raise so that it looks like a porcupine.

The rat also may be mimicking another African animal, a weasel-like creature called the zorilla. Like the rat, the zorilla is nocturnal. It is also black and white and raises its fur when threatened. The zorilla can spray terrible-smelling fluid, just like a skunk. The rat cannot spray, but when it stiffens its mane, it exposes patches of skin bordered with white. Glands in the skin release a strong, foul smell. Few predators tackle either the zorilla or the rat.

People who live in the maned rat's range believe that the rat's glands also produce poison. Scientists don't yet know if this is true. If it is, the rat would be considered a Müllerian mimic—a harmful animal that resembles other harmful animals.

MÜLLERIAN MIMICS

Some of the insects that mimic bad-smelling, inedible lycid bee-tles are harmless Batesian mimics. However, lycid beetles also have mimics that are just as sickening to predators. These mimics include bad-tasting beetles and moths as well as stinging wasps. They are all Müllerian mimics—harmful animals that mimic other harmful animals. Müllerian mimics are also called "co-mimics."

It may seem strange for an animal that has defenses of its own to mimic another animal. A stinging wasp and a nauseating moth, both with warning colors, can easily educate predators to leave them alone without mimicking a nasty beetle. This kind of mimicry, however, may have developed because it benefits the models as well as the mimics. They share the task of educating predators, and they also share the danger of being caught by a predator that has not yet learned to leave them alone.

The colorful *Heliconius* butterflies of tropical Central and South America are among the best examples of Müllerian mimicry at work. There are more than 40 species of *Heliconius* butterflies. As caterpillars, they feed on the vines of poisonous passion plants. Their bodies become poisonous. Later, they grow to be poisonous butterflies with black, red-orange, and yellow-ish wings. The butterflies also give off strong smells, which may help warn predators that rely on smell more than sight. *Heliconius* butterflies of different species resemble each other, so predators that learn to avoid one species will then avoid similar-looking butterflies of other species. The butterflies employ Müllerian mimicry across the range of places in which they live. Butterflies of one *Heliconius* species in a particular place may look different from butterflies of the same species in another place, but their co-mimics look different in each place, too.

Heliconius butterflies, in turn, are mimicked by butterflies that are not related to them. Some of these butterflies may also

Heliconius hecale butterflies may look different in different areas, but their co-mimics also look similar in each of those areas.

be poisonous, but others are not. Some are not butterflies at all, but day-flying moths.

The links among these insects are so complex that scientists put them in groups based on colors, not by kinds: "tiger," "red," "blue," "orange," and "transparent." These groups are called mimicry rings.

Species of poisonous burnet moths also wear warning colors in different patterns of red, black, yellow, and white. These day-flying moths are found in much of Europe, Africa, and Asia. Their bodies make a strong acid that's carried in their blood. Species of burnet moths living in the same area look similar to one another. They share their habitat with unrelated poisonous moths that look similar, too.

Pacific beetle cockroaches are also Müllerian mimics. These cockroaches spray a foul-smelling fluid from the sides of their bodies at ants and other predators. They look and smell like darkling beetles, which tip forward when threatened to spray a

CATERPILLARS THAT MIMIC SNAKES

From a predator's point of view, caterpillars are packaged meals—soft-bodied, protein-packed morsels. Ants, birds, monkeys, and other animals feed on them. Caterpillars have evolved a wide array of defenses to repel them. Snake mimicry is one of these defenses.

Many caterpillars, moths, and butterflies have patches of bright color shaped like eyes that can be flashed at a predator. The sudden appearance of eyespots can startle a bird or a similar predator long enough to delay its attack and give the insect time to escape. Eyespots also help some caterpillars pull off a convincing imitation of a snake.

The caterpillar of an elephant hawk-moth, for example, has a scaly pattern on its body and big eyespots near its head. When it is threatened, it tucks in its head, which makes its eyespots bulge. Suddenly, the caterpillar appears to be a watchful snake.

Another hawk-moth caterpillar found in South America mimics a tree-dwelling viper. It turns into a snake by relaxing its grip on a branch and raising its front end. Then it puffs up its body just behind its head and turns sideways.

(continues)

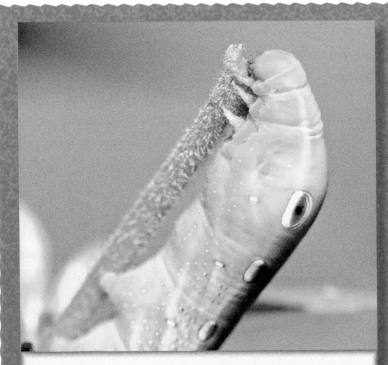

The tiger swallowtail caterpillar can trick predators with its large eyespots.

(continued)

These actions make the front of the caterpillar look like a triangular snake head, complete with eyes, scales, and small pits found on the face of a viper. The caterpillar will even jab at a predator as if it were going to bite.

Caterpillars of some swallowtail butterflies also seem to mimic snakes. A swallowtail caterpillar's plump front end sports large eyespots that look as if they are staring directly at a predator. This visual trick works even if the predator moves from one side of the caterpillar to the other or sneaks behind it. Some scientists, however, think these caterpillars may be mimicking bad-tasting tree frogs instead.

stinky fluid. They are often called "stink beetles" as a result. (A Batesian mimic, the cactus longhorn beetle, copies the darkling beetle's behavior but does not have any smelly spray.)

THE MONARCH BUTTERFLY'S STORY

Scientists are studying mimicry in many insects and other animals. They are studying bumblebees, plant-sucking bugs, poison dart frogs, sea slugs, sea cucumbers, and flatworms, as well as other butterflies and moths. In recent years, scientists found that one of the most common examples of a Batesian model and mimic was wrong. This pair consists of the monarch butterfly and the viceroy butterfly.

The monarch is a beautiful orange, black, and white butterfly of North, South, and Central America. It feeds on poisonous milkweed plants as a caterpillar. It is unharmed by the poison and stores it up in its body to make itself poisonous to predators.

The monarch (*left*) and viceroy (*right*) butterflies are now thought to be part of a group of Müllerian mimics—harmful animals that mimic other harmful animals.

This protection lasts into adulthood. Birds that grab monarchs quickly drop them, or throw them up if they have already swallowed them. Studies show that such birds refuse to eat monarchs or their look-alikes again.

One of the monarch's look-alikes is the viceroy butterfly. For more than 100 years, the viceroy was thought to be a Batesian mimic of the monarch: tasty, but avoided by birds because of how it looked. In 1991, scientists put an idea to the test. They removed the wings from dead butterflies, including some monarchs and viceroys, then fed the bodies to red-winged blackbirds. The experiment showed that the birds found the viceroys just as nasty-tasting as the monarchs.

The viceroy and the monarch are now thought to be part of a group of Müllerian mimics that includes the monarch's relatives, the soldier butterfly and the queen butterfly.

7

Fighting Back

A BULL MOOSE grazing in a field suddenly jerks up his head. He senses that wolves are nearby. Ears pricked, nostrils flared, he stares in the wolves' direction.

The wolves stare back. They had quietly stalked the moose for nearly half an hour. Once they got close, they intended to do what wolves always do when hunting: charge full speed at the moose. This rush usually made prey run away so the wolves could chase it.

Not this time. They had lost the advantage of surprise. The alert moose had sensed them. He did not run, but stood his ground and continued to return their stare.

The moose, without moving a muscle, is sending the wolves many signals. By standing his ground and looking at them, he warns the predators that they have been seen, and that he is more than a match for them.

The wolves are aware of this. They have speed, strength, and sharp fangs, but the moose is also well equipped for self-defense. The massive antlers on his head are the least of their worries—a bull moose mainly uses the antlers to battle other bull moose— but his hard, sharp hooves are deadly. The wolves know that a powerful kick from a hind hoof or a slashing kick from a front hoof could injure or kill one of them.

The moose takes a step toward the wolves. The wolves turn around and glide back into the woods, giving up the hunt. They will search for easier prey.

Though wolf and moose are hunter and hunted, they are alike in one way: Both species defend themselves with body parts that are mainly used for other, non-defensive purposes. These body parts did not evolve primarily as weapons for defense. The wolf's teeth, for example, are tools for killing prey and eating meat. The moose's hooves are for running, and his antlers are for male-to-male combat in mating season.

Many animals have evolved special body parts used for defense, such as stings, but many other animals defend themselves with body parts that have evolved for other activities: eating, digging, climbing, and the like.

Hunting together, the wolves were working as a group, a behavior that prey species also use to their advantage. Many species that live in herds, flocks, schools, or other groups cooperate in defense. This defense may consist of sounding an alarm, posting a lookout, or working together to repel a predator. In some insect species, individual insects even develop into specially formed workers called soldiers.

TEETH AND TUSKS

Animals use their teeth mainly for eating. Yet, animals primarily thought of as predators—such as lions, wolves, and other large **carnivores**—have sharp teeth and fangs for killing prey and shearing meat from bones. These predators usually have strong jaws, too. A hyena's jaws can crush the leg bone of a zebra. Smaller predators use their sharp teeth to kill prey.

Plant-eating animals, or herbivores, have teeth adapted for feeding on plants. Horses' teeth push up slowly out of their jaw-bones during their entire lives. This is to replace the top parts that wear down from grazing. A deer has nipping teeth in the front of its lower jaw and a tough pad on the top jaw, which it uses to rip leaves off plants. Molars in the back are used for chewing. Rodents have front teeth that grow continuously throughout their lives. Elephants have several sets of teeth, with new sets moving in from the back to replace worn-out ones in front.

Teeth also make good weapons. Many animals, such as lions, tigers, dogs, bears, and badgers, show their teeth and growl if

The sharp tusks of a hippopotamus can be used as a weapon. Here, a hippo marks its territory by opening its mouth—a behavior seen mainly during mating season.

threatened. Some grazing animals, such as horses and zebras, bite attackers. Mice, rabbits, and other small animals also bite if they are caught.

Animals with special long teeth called tusks are equipped with dangerous weapons. An elephant's two front teeth are tusks, which may stick out of the mouth. The tusks of a male African elephant can be up to 8 feet (2.4 m) long. Elephants use their tusks to dig water holes, scrape bark off trees, and spar with each other. They also use them as weapons against lions and other animals that prey on their calves.

Hippopotamuses use their long, razor-sharp lower teeth as weapons. A hippo tusk can grow up to 20 inches (51 cm) long. Males bite each other while fighting. Females use their tusks to keep males away from their babies. If a predator comes near a calf, the mother hippo will attack it, too. A hippo can kill a lion, and can even bite a crocodile in half.

Another African animal, the warthog, has four tusks. Two sharp tusks jut from the lower jaw, and two more curl from the upper jaw. Warthogs use these tusks to dig up roots to eat. Male warthogs also use the blunt, curled tusks when they fight one another. If a lion threatens a warthog, the warthog runs away or dives backward into a burrow, with its tusked snout facing outward.

CLAWS, HOOVES, AND PINCERS

A threatened animal with legs—two, four, or more—is most likely to use them to escape. But if it is cornered or caught, an animal will use its legs and feet to defend itself.

An animal with clawed toes, such as a cat or raccoon, kicks and scratches to defend itself. It may also bite at the same time. A kangaroo not only bites and punches with its clawed front feet, but also leans back on its tail to kick with its hind legs. Then it slashes downward with the sharp claws on its big hind feet.

Birds, such as chickens, will claw and peck as they struggle to escape. A large bird can also kick at its foe. An ostrich, for example, kicks forward at its attacker. Then it slashes downward to rake it with its sharp claws, which measure up to 4 inches (10 cm) long. An ostrich's kick is powerful enough to kill a lion.

Hoofed animals also kick to ward off attackers. A giraffe can kill its only predator, the lion, with a single kick. A zebra kicks out with its hind legs at a predator chasing it and can break its jaw or neck. Deer kick at coyotes with their front hooves.

Many animals lack claws or hooves, but can use other appendages to defend themselves. A lobster has large claws called pincers that it uses to catch and crush crabs, clams, and other prey. It also uses them to defend itself. A lobster's pinching power is strong enough to break a person's finger joint. Crabs can pinch hard enough to draw blood. Insects that cannot sting will often bite—sometimes painfully.

HORNS AND ANTLERS

Many kinds of hoofed animals grow horns or antlers on their heads. Horns are bones that grow out of the skulls of sheep, goats, cattle, and antelope, such as gazelles. These bones are covered by a layer of tough material called horn. Horned animals do not shed their horns. Antlers also are made of bone, but they fall off and grow again each year. Unlike horns, antlers divide into branches.

At first glance, a deer's antlers look like weapons for self-defense, but they are used more for interacting with other deer. Their use as weapons against predators is not their main purpose.

Although antlers may seem like a good weapon, a deer typically uses its antlers more for interacting with other deer than for fighting off predators.

Male deer of most species grow antlers, while females do not. The males use their antlers in battles with other males over females. In these battles, the males shove their antlered heads against each other and jab at each other's sides. Female reindeer and caribou do grow antlers, but they shed them later in the year than males do. The females use antlers to keep other herd members out of the feeding holes they have scraped in the snow.

Horns grow on both males and females in many species of goat, sheep, cattle, and antelope. Males use their horns to battle with other males over females. They also use horns as weapons for self-defense. Females use their horns to defend themselves and their young against predators. Females of large species of antelope are more likely to have horns than females of smaller species. These smaller species tend to hide and use camouflage for protection.

Both male and female rhinoceroses have horns on their faces. Asian rhinos have one horn. African rhinos have two. These horns are not made of bone. They are made of keratin—the same material found in fingernails, toenails and hair.

Male rhinos use their horns in battles with one another. Both males and females will also charge at intruders. Predators, such as lions, are not willing to tackle a grown rhino, but they do try to catch calves. The white rhino, an African species, can protect a calf simply by standing still with the baby hiding under her huge, two-horned head.

GROUP DEFENSE

Many animals find safety in numbers by living in large groups. Bison live in herds. Tuna and many other fish species form large schools. Geese and other birds form flocks as they **migrate** from one place to another when the seasons change. Aphids cluster together on stems.

Living in a group helps animals defend themselves against predators in several ways. Lone animals must rely only on their own senses, but an animal in a group benefits by having lots of other animals' eyes, ears, and noses on the alert for danger. An animal in a group also has a smaller chance of being the unlucky individual picked out by a predator.

In addition, a group of animals fleeing from a predator can create confusion. This makes it harder for a predator to focus on one animal to catch. A school of fish will split in two to avoid a predator, and then quickly regroup behind it. A herd of zebras can become a dazzling display of black and white stripes, making it more difficult for a lion to see where one zebra ends and another begins. Starlings clump together when a hawk approaches. This makes it harder for the hawk to single out one bird.

Animal groups may be made up of just one species. Striped coral-reef catfish, for example, travel in a dense, ball-shaped school when they are young. Many seabirds nest in crowded colonies on islands and gang up on trespassing predators.

Animals may also form mixed groups, such as the herds of hoofed animals that migrate across Africa's plains. There, shaggy horned animals called gnus form herds of up to one million animals. Traveling along with them are tens of thousands of zebras and gazelles.

Groups of animals also may work together to drive off a predator. One of the most famous examples of group defense is the circle formed by musk oxen. Musk oxen are huge, shaggy cattle that live on the broad, snowy lands of the Arctic known as the tundra. Females and young live in herds year-round. Males join these herds for part of the year.

If wolves attack a herd, musk oxen form a circle with their calves in the middle and their horns facing out. The wolves face a wall of horns backed up by hundreds of pounds of muscle. Musk oxen also will rush out and try to hook a wolf with their horns.

Scientists have seen other animals, such as gnus and white rhinos, form defensive circles.

Zebras do not form circles, but small herds do work together to foil predators. If a pack of hyenas creeps up on a herd, a male zebra charges at them, ready to bite and kick. The females and young gather together and move away. Often a female known as the lead mare guides them. Wild horses also behave in this way. Other animals, such as elephants and cattle, approach and threaten predators that come near their herds.

Large African monkeys called baboons also live in groups. They sometimes work together to drive off predators. Scientists have seen males of one species of baboon ganging up on leopards and dogs to chase them away. A smaller monkey, the red colobus, also teams up with other males to defend their group when chimpanzees attack. The male monkeys get between the females and their young and the chimps. They leap onto the chimps and bite them.

Many species of small, burrowing mammals cooperate against predators, too. These animals alert each other to danger. Meerkats are weasel-like animals that live in dry lands of southern Africa. When they leave their burrows to look for food, a few animals stand guard. The guards climb onto a rock or a termite mound and stand on their hind legs. They scan the skies for eagles and hawks. They also keep an eye out for hungry jackals. If a predator appears, the guards call quickly and sharply. This is the signal for everybody to dive into the burrows.

North American prairie dogs, which are related to squirrels, also live in burrows. The burrows cover a huge area of land known as a prairie-dog town. Prairie dogs do not post guards. Yet, because there are so many prairie dogs, someone in the town is likely to spot a hawk or a coyote. Prairie dogs that spot danger will give a danger call. At this signal, everybody scurries underground to safety.

This meerkat in the Kalahari Desert of South Africa stands guard atop a rock, ready to call out a warning if predators approach.

ALARM SIGNALS

Meerkats and prairie dogs are just two of the many animals that give alarm calls when they see predators. Scientists have found that many kinds of animals give alarm calls. These animals often give different calls for different predators. The animals that hear the alarms behave in different ways for each call.

Florida scrub jays take turns being on guard duty while the rest of the family group feeds. When a scrub jay sees a predator, it gives an alarm call. It makes a high-pitched scream if it sees a hawk, and a sharp cawing sound if it sees a cat. The alarm call warns other birds of danger. It also tells the predator that it has been spotted.

Little birds called black-capped chickadees also send coded alarm calls. If a chickadee sees a flying predator, such as a hawk, it makes a soft, high-pitched call. This tells other birds to hide. Other calls are used to warn of predators that are perched on a branch or on the ground. These calls warn other birds that a predator is near, and even tell them how dangerous it is.

MOBBING BY BIRDS

Many species of birds will gang up on a predator and bother it when it is not hunting. This behavior is called mobbing.

Crows will gather around an eagle perched in a tree and caw at it. They will even fly close to it and strike it in passing. Their caws attract more crows that will join in the attack. The crows mob the eagle until it flies away. Small birds mob predators, too. A mob may be made up of birds of several species.

Scientists who study birds have long wondered why birds would risk their lives to mob a hawk, cat, fox, or other predator, especially one that is not hunting. They have come up with several reasons.

The mobbing birds may be letting the predator know that it has been seen, so it might as well go hunt somewhere else. They may be parent birds trying to distract the predator so that it will not look for their nests. They may be trying to get the attention of a bigger predator—one that will go after the birds' predator. Mobbing also helps other birds know that there is a predator in the neighborhood.

One Florida scrub jay will look for predators while the family group eats. If it spots danger, it calls out an alarm warning so the others can flee.

A chickadee that sees a small owl perched in a tree, for example, adds extra "dee" sounds to the end of its "chick-a-dee" call. These extra sounds warn other chickadees that a very dangerous predator is in the area. A big owl gets one extra "dee." This is because the small owl is quick enough to catch a chickadee, but the big owl is not; it is more likely to hunt for mice and rats.

Some mammals, such as meerkats, also communicate information about predators with their alarm calls. A meerkat on guard duty peeps quietly to let others know that everything is fine. If it sees an eagle, it gives a call that sends meerkats scurrying into burrows. If it sees a snake, it gives a call that tells other meerkats to climb trees instead. Yet another call tells other meerkats to mob a less-dangerous predator and chase it away.

Vervet monkeys, found in Africa, have one call that means a big cat, such as a leopard, is near. This call tells other vervets to climb high up into a tree. Another call means an eagle is overhead. This causes monkeys to hide in a bush or among the branches of a tree. A third call means "snake." Monkeys stand up on their hind legs and look around carefully when they hear this call.

Other species of monkey—as well as ground squirrels, tree squirrels, and lemurs—also use different calls for different predators. Scientists have also found that one species' alarm call may be understood by other species. Many animals flee when they hear other animals get excited or alarmed, but some animals appear to understand the details of the alarm. Little birds called nuthatches know when a chickadee's alarm call means "little owl" and when it means "big owl."

Not all alarm signals are calls. Alarm signals can also be seen, smelled, or otherwise sensed. An alarmed black-tail deer raises its tail and the hair on its rump. A patch of skin on its hind leg also releases a strong odor. The pronghorn, an antelope-like animal of western North America, also raises long, white hairs on its rump and releases a scent from its musk glands.

Insects also use smells as alarm signals. Pheromones are scents and other chemicals used for communication. Bees, wasps, and ants produce pheromones when they sting. The pheromones alert other insects, which come to help defend the nest. An insect called a lace bug protects her eggs and young by fluttering her wings at beetles. If her defense fails and a larva is grabbed, she produces a pheromone that warns the other larvae to flee. Likewise, an aphid attacked by a predator makes a fluid that not only clogs up the predator's mouth, but also contains a pheromone that causes other aphids to dash away.

Underwater animals use pheromones as alarm signals, too. A sea anemone that is nibbled by a fish gives off a pheromone that makes nearby anemones close up. Many fish, such as minnows, release pheromones when a predator injures them. Fish that pick up the scent will hide or swim away.

BEES, WASPS, ANTS, AND TERMITES

Some insects live and work together to raise the colony's young. These animals are called social insects. Among the social insects are honeybees, wasps, ants, and termites.

Honeybees live in a colony made up of one queen and thousands of workers. The workers all have stings and use them to defend the colony. A honeybee's sting pulls out of its body and remains in the victim's skin, so the bee dies after it stings. A gland near the sting releases pheromones, which bring other bees to help in the defense.

Some species of wasps also form colonies. Yellow jackets raise their young inside large, papery nests. They will swarm out of a nest to attack an intruder. Paper wasps also build nests. A paper-wasp queen attacks intruders with even more energy than her workers. Like bees, social wasps send out chemical alarms when they sting. Some wasp species, however, defend only themselves and not the nest.

All ants live in colonies and defend them. An animal that noses around a fire-ant colony's nest will quickly find itself facing a swarm of ants pouring out, ready to bite.

Some species of ants have special "soldier" ants that work as security guards for the nest. A soldier may be larger than the average worker ant. It also has bigger jaws. In some species, the soldiers have extra-sharp jaws. In others, the soldiers have heads shaped like shields. They use their heads to plug the nest's entrance holes to keep out invaders. Leafcutter ants are guarded by larger soldiers when they leave the nest to gather leaves. They also are guarded by tiny worker ants that perch on their backs. The worker ants watch out for wasps that try to lay eggs on the workers.

Like ants, termites live in colonies. Workers and soldiers take care of a queen as well as a king termite. Termite soldiers defend the colony. They typically have thick, strong heads and large jaws for biting.

Soldiers of some termite species spew a sticky spray from their nozzle-shaped heads. The spray irritates ants that get hit. The soldiers march alongside the worker termites to guard them when they go outside to gather food. Some termite species lack soldiers, but the workers have a strange ability: They explode, covering their enemies with their sticky insides.

ONGOING ADAPTATIONS

Today, animals continue to adapt to their environment and to the other living things that share their habitat. Prey animals evolve behaviors and traits that help defend them against predators, while predators evolve to get around their prey's defenses. This back-and-forth between predator and prey is often referred to as a "biological arms race."

USING HEAT IN SELF-DEFENSE

Rattlesnakes and some other snakes can find prey by sensing the heat it produces. Recently, scientists have found that one kind of prey, the California ground squirrel, uses its body heat to defend itself against these snakes.

An alarmed ground squirrel waves its tail to make itself seem larger. This can help it fend off a snake. If the snake senses heat, however, the squirrel also causes its tail to grow warmer. This makes the squirrel's "heat image" look larger to the snake. These squirrels do not heat up their tails unless the snake is a species that can sense heat.

Japanese honeybees also use heat as a defense. Giant hornets raid the bees' nests to eat the honey. Then they carry the young, still-growing bees back to their nests to feed to their own young.

The hornets' attack begins with one "scout" hornet, which marks the bees' nest with a pheromone. The pheromone lures dozens of other hornets to the nest to carry out the raid.

European honeybees imported to Japan try to fight back by stinging, but the hornets kill them all in just a few hours. Japanese honeybees, however, have evolved a way to kill the hornets. When a scout hornet arrives, up to 500 bees swarm around it. They vibrate their bodies to produce heat. The temperature rises inside the cluster of bees. The bees can stand the heat, but it is too hot for the hornet: It bakes to death before it gets a chance to spread its pheromones on the nest.

In many cases, new predators introduced into a species' habitat cause this arms race to escalate. Often, prey animals cannot keep up. Many birds that nest on islands, for example, are not well defended against land predators. No such predators lived on their islands, so they did not need to evolve defensive behaviors against them. Human visitors to these islands brought predators such as cats and rats. In some places, these predators have nearly wiped out the defenseless island animals.

Scientists who research predator-prey relationships learn not only about the history and evolution of the animals' behaviors, but also about their future. Recent studies seem to show that when predators become extinct in an area, the prey animals often start losing their defense behaviors. For example, moose living in places where predators had been hunted to extinction did not act like moose living where predators were plentiful. Moose living in places with no wolves were alarmed when they smelled wolves, but they showed only mild interest and did not leave the area.

In places where wolves had returned, however, moose began to show defense behaviors over time. They started becoming alarmed when they heard wolves howl. In one park where bears had returned, female moose began having their calves close to roadways, where the bears would not approach them.

Prey animals have learned to use humans and their constructions as "safe harbors" in other places. Vervet monkeys in parts of Africa hang out near ranger stations, where leopards do not go. In Nepal, deer likewise find safety from tigers by staying near a tourist center.

As scientists research animal behavior, they continue to find new behaviors. They also find clues that shed light on past observations of animal behavior. These discoveries help increase understanding of predators and prey and how they interact. The knowledge gained may help scientists and others consider how human activities, such as development and fishing, affect these complex systems.

Glossary

Adaptations Behaviors, body shapes, and other features that help a species survive and reproduce

Aposematism Colors, smells, behaviors, and other adaptations that prey use to warn predators

Batesian mimicry A form of mimicry in which a harmless animal resembles a poisonous, venomous, or otherwise harmful animal

Carnivore An animal that uses its sharp teeth to kill and eat its prey

Chain mail A kind of armor made from small metal rings linked together

Crypsis The ability of an animal to avoid being noticed by predators or other animals

Deflection display A color, body part, or behavior that distracts a predator and fools it into attacking a part of its prey, such as the tail, that is not vital to the prey's survival

Evolution The process in which a population of living things changes over time

Exoskeleton The outer, hard covering of an insect or other invertebrate

Eyespots Patterns on an animal's body that look like eyes and are used to startle and frighten predators

Flash coloration Hidden colors on an animal's body that are suddenly revealed in order to startle and distract a predator

Invertebrate An animal that does not have a backbone

Masking   A defense behavior in which an animal camouflages it-self by carrying or attaching items, such as leaves or seaweed, to its body

Migrate   To travel long distances at certain times of the year. For example, monarch butterflies migrate south for the winter

Mimic   A species that predators may avoid because it looks like another species that's poisonous, bad tasting, or bad smelling

Model   A species that is mimicked by at least one other species

Müllerian mimicry   A form of mimicry in which a harmful species mimics another harmful species

Nematocysts   The stingers of cnidarians, which include ocean animals such as corals, anemones, and jellyfish

Pheromones   Chemicals produced by an animal that affect the behavior of other animals belonging to the same species

Predator   An animal that eats other animals

Prey   An animal that is eaten by other animals

Primary defenses   Defenses that an animal has all the time, such as camouflage or spiky skin

Reflex bleeding   When an insect oozes blood from its joints to confuse or distract a predator

Scutes   Tough scales that are found in the skin of reptiles and the shells of most turtles and tortoises

Secondary defenses   Defenses, such as biting or spraying musk, used only after an animal has been detected or attacked by a predator

Startle display   An animal's use of body parts, colors, or behaviors to startle a predator. This gives the prey more time to escape.

Venom   Poisonous substances that animals make and inject into other animals using stings, fangs, or other body parts

Vertebrate   An animal with a backbone

Bibliography

Agosta, William. *Bombardier Beetles and Fever Trees: A Close-Up Look at Chemical Warfare and Signals in Animals and Plants*. New York: Addison-Wesley Publishing Company, 1996.

Allen, Thomas B., Karen Jensen, and Philip Kopper. *Earth's Amazing Animals*. Washington, D.C.: National Wildlife Federation, 1983.

Bauchot, Roland, ed. *Snakes: A Natural History*. New York: Sterling Publishing Co., Inc., 1993.

"The Birds and the Beetles." Smithsonian National Zoological Park Web Site. Available online. URL: http://nationalzoo.si.edu/ConservationAndScience/SpotlightOnScience/dumbacherj20041129.cfm.

Birkhead, Mike, and Tim Birkhead. *The Survival Factor*. New York: Facts On File, 1990.

Burton, Robert. *Venomous Animals*. New York: Crescent Books, 1978.

Cloudsley-Thompson, J.L. *Tooth and Claw: Defensive Strategies in the Animal World*. London: J.M. Dent & Sons, Ltd., 1980.

Dozier, Thomas A. *Dangerous Sea Creatures*. New York: Time-Life Films, 1977.

Eisner, Thomas. *For Love of Insects*. Cambridge, Mass.: The Belknap Press of Harvard University Press, 2003.

———. Secret *Weapons: Defenses of Insects, Spiders, Scorpions, and Other Many-Legged Creatures*. Cambridge, Mass.: The Belknap Press of Harvard University Press, 2005.

Fogden, Michael, and Patricia Fogden. *Animals and Their Colors*. New York: Crown Publishers, Inc., 1974.

Galan, Mark. *Animal Behavior*. Alexandria, Va.: Time-Life Books, 1991.

Hartup, Wendi. "Do Venomous Caterpillars Live in Your Yard?" Forsyth County Cooperative Extension Web Site. Available online. URL: http://www.ca.uky.edu/entomology/entfacts/ef003.asp.

Lambeth, Ellen. "Animals in Armor: Having a Hard Body Is a Good Thing If You're an Animal Under Attack." *Ranger Rick* (May 1997).

Line, Les. "When the Best Offense Is a Good Defense." *National Wildlife* 41, no. 2 (February–March 2003).

Mattison, Chris. *The Encyclopedia of Snakes*. New York: Facts on File, 1995.

Morris, Desmond. *Animalwatching*. New York: Crown Publishers, 1990.

O'Toole, Christopher, ed. *The Encyclopedia of Insects*. New York: Facts on File, 1985.

Schwarz, Joel. "Chickadees' Alarm-calls Carry Information about Size, Threat of Predator." University of Washington Web Site. Available online. URL: http://uwnews.washington.edu/ni/article.asp?articleID_10732.

Sohn, Emily. "Toxic Birds May Get Poison from Beetles." *Science News for Kids* Web Site. Available online. URL: http://www.sciencenewsforkids.org/articles/20041110/Note2.asp.

Tanner, Ogden. *Animal Defenses*. New York: Time-Life Films, 1978.

Turner, Pamela S. "Who You Callin' 'Shrimp'?" *National Wildlife* 43, no. 6 (October–November 2005).

Further Resources

BOOKS

Castner, James L. *Surviving in the Rain Forest*. Tarrytown, N.Y.: Marshall Cavendish Corporation, 2002.

Ganeri, Anita. *Prickly and Poisonous*. Westport, Conn.: Reader's Digest Young Families, Inc., 1995.

Kafner, Etta, and Pat Stephens. *How Animals Defend Themselves*. Tonawanda, N.Y.: Kids Can Press Ltd., 2006.

Kalman, Bobbie, and John Crossingham. *What Are Camouflage and Mimicry?* New York: Crabtree Publishing Company, 2001.

Lovett, Sarah. *Extremely Weird Animal Defenses*. Santa Fe, N.M.: John Muir Publications, 1997.

Perry, Phyllis J. *Armor to Venom: Animal Defenses*. New York: Franklin Watts, 1997.

———. *Hide and Seek: Creatures in Camouflage*. New York: Franklin Watts, 1997.

Petty, Kate. *Animal Camouflage and Defense*. Langhorne, Pa.: Chelsea House Publishers, 2005.

Souza, D.M. *Packed with Poison! Deadly Animal Defenses*. Minneapolis, Minn.: Millbrook Press, 2006.

Wolfe, Art. *Vanishing Act*. New York: Bulfinch Press, 2005.

WEB SITES

National Geographic Society
http://kids.nationalgeographic.com/Animals/CreatureFeature/

The National Geographic Society's site offers in-depth profiles of animal species, including videos.

National Wildlife Federation
http://www.nwf.org/kids/

The National Wildlife Federation's site focuses on animals and the environment.

PBS's *Nature*
http://www.pbs.org/wnet/nature/critter.html

The Public Broadcasting Service's site based on the television program *Nature*; provides profiles of animals as well as activities and videos.

Science News for Kids
http://www.sciencenewsforkids.org/

News and articles about science topics, including animal behavior, as well as science-related activities, book suggestions, games, and puzzles; maintained by the Society for Science & the Public.

The Smithsonian National Zoological Park
http://nationalzoo.si.edu/Audiences/kids/

The Smithsonian National Zoological Park's site offers information about animals, puzzles, games, photographs, and Animal Cam access to view animals at the zoo.

Picture Credits

Index

131

About the Author

Christina Wilsdon is the author of many nonfiction books for young readers, as well as articles on natural history for adults. In her career, she has written regularly for *3-2-1 Contact*, *National Geographic World*, *Creative Classroom*, Reader's Digest Young Families, and the Audubon Society. In 1997 Wilsdon received an EdPress Distinguished Achievement Award for Excellence in Educational Journalism for an article about a zoo's composting program. She currently lives with her family in the Pacific Northwest, where she enjoys bird watching, especially in her garden.